HANS KLEIBER

Hans Kleiber

HANS KLEIBER:
ARTIST OF THE BIG
HORN MOUNTAINS

by

EMMIE D. MYGATT

and

ROBERTA CHENEY

THE CAXTON PRINTERS, LTD.
Caldwell, Idaho 83605
1975

Library of Congress Cataloging in Publication Data

Mygatt, Emmie D
    Hans Kleiber, artist of the Big Horn Mountains.

    1. Kleiber, Hans, 1887-1967. I. Cheney,
Roberta Carkeek, joint author. II. Kleiber,
Hans, 1887-1967. III. Title.
N6537.K55M94   760'.92'4   75-12294
ISBN 0-87004-247-5

Printed and bound in the United States of America by
The CAXTON PRINTERS, Ltd.
Caldwell, Idaho 83605
123189

This book is dedicated to the many friends of Hans Kleiber who helped him to become a successful artist and who now treasure his paintings and etchings and share his love of the Big Horn Country.

CONTENTS

ILLUSTRATIONS

PHOTOGRAPHS

PREFACE

Hans Kleiber knew that invaluable learning and living experience was concentrated in great cities, preserved and presented for man's use. Without great galleries, his own work would never have achieved wide recognition; without his brief learning experience in the New York area, his struggle for artistic expression would have been infinitely harder. He took what he needed from cities, but his natural life-style was not in harmony with urban living.

Kleiber never swerved from his belief that man cannot be really whole if he is completely cut off from nature, must always walk on cement, be enclosed by stone, and never feel earth beneath his feet.

The unusual man eventually fights his way through an improbable set of circumstances to the work for which he was intended. Hans Kleiber was such a man. At thirty-five he resigned from the U.S. Forest Service, where he had worked for almost two decades, to begin a new life as an artist. Practically self-taught, his talent and stamina allowed him to perpetuate the strength and tranquility he found in his mountains.

To look at a Hans Kleiber etching or watercolor on your own wall is a source of strength and joy, of remembered or distant beauty. But a picture on the wall is a privilege open only to a few. In this book, many are gathered. It is our hope that Hans Kleiber's ability to translate natural truth into visible form will make this volume a source of pleasure.

We have chosen to let Hans's own words, as well as his pictures, reveal the man. He left one published book of poems and voluminous notebooks full of reports, reminiscences, and stories. From these we have selected passages, sometimes only a sentence, sometimes a whole story or poem. No amount of rewriting or trying to portray Hans Kleiber in our own words was as effective as letting him speak for himself through the manuscripts that he left.

This book is not so much an account of his life as a glimpse into the experiences which served as background and inspiration for his art. To that end we have selected passages that encompass each facet of his interests, personal contacts, influences, and above all his feelings and aspirations.

Kleiber's paintings and etchings are not photographic; he has injected his sensitive vision of trees, birds, and animals into their portrayal. Much of what he saw when it was fresh and unspoiled is now endangered. In that sense this book is a timely one. Whatever may happen to his Big Horn country, Hans has preserved it at its best and left it for others to enjoy.

The authors also feel that Hans's unique quality as a man should not be lost. For twenty-five years, at first only in summers, Ken and Emmie Mygatt were privileged to share a close and joyous friendship with Hans and his second wife, Missie. It also happened that Emmie was with Hans during the last hour of his life.

An artist's fame grows after his death. It was inevitable that books about Hans Kleiber would be written. We wanted at least one to come from a source of personal recollection supplemented by careful historical research which was accomplished by Roberta Cheney.

ACKNOWLEDGEMENTS

We are deeply grateful to Stuart and Kay Kleiber who turned over to us all of Hans Kleiber's notebooks and journals and allowed us to choose etchings for this book from their collection. We are also indebted to John Patton for use of his complete collection of etchings, and to Tucker's Store in Sheridan who made etchings available to us, and to the people who loaned their original oils and watercolors to us for reproduction.

We particularly appreciate the artistic evaluation by Dr. James Forrest, museum director, art professor at the University of Wyoming and a close personal friend of Hans Kleiber during the artist's later years.

EDM
RCC

PART ONE

HIS BOYHOOD

4

In every boy a future man is hidden — to be carved out by his environment and by choices made as the youngster develops. The rare one rejects experiences that do not lead him to his goal and unconsciously absorbs everything that will take him to his destination. Hans Kleiber was such a boy. His love of natural things broke through every obstacle and not only predetermined his character but also the form his art would take.

His road was not easy, nor did it lead directly to his goal. He must have been born, as most children are, with a sense of wonder and of being one with all nature. Too many youngsters lose these perceptions at an early age, but Hans never did. As the story of his adventurous life unfolds, one realizes how deeply each one of his pictures was lived before he etched or painted it.

Hans Kleiber was born August 24, 1887, while his parents were traveling in Germany. When Hans was a few months old, the family returned to Jaegersdorf, their ancestral home. At that time it was a part of the old Austro-Hungarian Empire. Jaegersdorf was a fair-sized industrial town on the east slope of the Sudeten Mountains. Hans's father was a textile designer with unusual and varied outside interests.

Left: Mountain and stream near Dinwoodie Peak

Kleiber's background was multilingual. German was his native tongue; French was mandatory in the schools, Polish optional. The Czechs were right next door. But Hans later came to speak English without an accent, unless it might have been a western one.

His recollections of early youth are so vivid that they are best told in his own words. The following quotes have been selected from the accounts he wrote.

While my childhood days in Silesia now seem as remote as though they had been lived on another planet, I feel that they influenced my entire life to such an extent that their outstanding features deserve to be mentioned.

My earliest memories date back to when I must have been about two years old and were of Mother holding me in her lap during the twilight hours while she sang or told stories to me, within easy reach of a red painted cradle holding a little sister. My main reason for snuggling close to her was that during her occasional absences our nursemaid, a peasant girl, had entertained me with all sorts of folk tales about wolves, dragons, robbers, witches, goblins, elves, dwarfs, and other mysterious beings. Some of these creatures were good and kind, others just mischievous, but many were wicked and cruel and had to be avoided at all costs, especially at night when they were on the prowl. So it wasn't surprising that I had grown afraid of the dark and always felt relieved when Mother gathered us to her and began to sing. As I discovered later on, she really had a very true and sweet voice. Her songs and stories always soothed whatever troubles beset me. Even after I had gone to school for two or three years and was no longer afraid of the dark, I often begged her to sing for us.

Although my mother loved being out of doors, she seldom took us to the city park in Jaegersdorf—a large and beautiful one — except to hear a concert now and then. She definitely preferred nature under less cultivated conditions. [So did Hans.]

There was little of logic or reasoning in her make-up, and I feel that most of my mother's reactions to whatever situations she faced during her life had their roots in intuition and impulse. But she had a heart full of love for her family, and, in spite of the storms and misfortunes she had to weather later on, that love remained. She was always doing something around the home or for others away from it, and it was never done half-heartedly. That was her way until she suddenly died one bitterly cold winter afternoon in Wyoming.

One of the most memorable features of our family life was that Father and Mother read aloud a great deal to one another, not only at home but on picnics as well, beside some woodland spring or stream. Father must have been rather good at it, for often when friends were along he would be asked to read passages of prose or poetry from a little volume he usually carried in his pocket. But while they were listening to him, I all too often wandered off into the woods to do a little exploring on my own, which on more than one occasion suddenly ended the reading and threw the party into a panic. Sooner or later I was always found by Father, who seemed to know instinctively where to look for me.

Another of Hans's earliest memories shows an intense curiosity about nature, even her fury:

The first storm to leave a lasting impression on me was when I was about three or four years old. It broke on a Sunday. My parents were out and I had been left in our apartment with a maid. I was sitting on a window seat to watch the people passing by, when the sun suddenly disappeared and a peal of thunder shook the house and rattled everything in it. The maid rushed up to drag me away, but I stubbornly refused to leave my perch — spellbound by the spectacle that was unfolding with terrifying speed. It reached its climax when a double bolt of lightning struck one of the church spires nearby. The girl began to sob beside me, praying and crying over and over again, 'Why, oh why, must our Heavenly

Frightened geese

Father strike down one of his own houses!' She did not stop crying until the last peal was but a distant rumble and the sun shone again. When my parents returned they shared my excitement and wonder.

In looking back on those early years in Silesia, I feel that our circumstances must have been fairly prosperous, for besides an apartment in the city Father always rented some peasant's cottage for the summer. In these villages ancient farmsteads and white-washed churches were strung along the larger streams. From them the meadows, fields, and pastures stretched up the gently rising slopes of the valleys until they became lost in the evergreen forests of the Sudeten Mountains, which extended west and northward as far as the eye could see. Compared to our forests on this side of the Atlantic, they had a cultivated look, because forestry had been practiced there for centuries.

Since Father and Mother shared a deep love for nature, we often went on long walking trips by ourselves or with friends visiting with us. Very early in life, these summer vacation days and trips into the woods instilled in me an abiding love and reverence for all that forests and mountains had to offer mankind. And what deepened that love even more was that my parents passed so much of it on to me. Few things escaped their notice; they commented on

A Swallowtail

Winter in Wyoming I

9

Storm

trees, flowers, grasses or whatever we happened to run into, large or small, that walked, fluttered, crawled, or swam, down to the rock outcrops and pebbles along our paths or in the streams.

As I grew older I was continuously surprised that Father, who had been brought up in a city, had such an inexhaustible fund of nature lore and knowledge. He was also highly sensitive to the aesthetic side of nature and never missed an opportunity to impress me with it. I often feel that those summer days in the Sudeten Mountains played their part in my falling in love with the Big Horns in Wyoming from the moment I laid eyes on them.

It wasn't until some years later that I began to understand fully how kind, unassuming, and just my father was, and to appreciate his inherent leanings toward the fine arts and literature. How he ever withstood the rough and tumble of his professional and administrative career as long as he did has always been a mystery to me. I recall finding him sitting alone in a chair after he came from work, with his head in his hands, sobbing quietly to himself. This was the aftermath, as Mother later confided to me, of an associate, friend or even a distant relative abusing his trust. He seldom spoke of himself, past or present, unless he thought of some particularly amusing incident, but never about the cares or troubles of his position. These he shared only with Mother. It was she who suggested they go to the United States when it had become apparent to her that his administrative responsibilities were more than he could bear for long. My father was, by natural endowments, a talented textile designer and widely recognized as such, but he was not a business man. My heart has bled for him many times since, for he dearly loved his native land and the people in it. This must have cost him no end of soul-searching before he could make up his mind to leave them forever.

While Mother had been reared in the Roman Catholic faith, my father was an atheist, a belief he never recanted nor wore on his sleeve. This may have been the reason why religious matters were seldom discussed in our home. There was nothing particularly pious in the observances of Mother's religious devotions; she took me to church every once in a while when I was a boy. The first time we went it must have been between services, for the church was silent and empty except for an old lady saying her devotions.

Mother stopped in a dark side nave before a dimly lighted huge oil painting of Mother Mary and her family, where, after making obeisances, she knelt with elbows on a low railing and her hands folded, praying almost inaudibly for a long time. She had motioned me to kneel beside her through her prayers, and I kept looking wonderingly at her face and lips and then to the Virgin's dimly lighted picture and back to my mother. Another time we went to a high mass when the church was crowded; lighted candles shone everywhere; the peals of the organ reverberated through the transept like thunder; a choir was singing; the priests were chanting, and clouds of incense almost hid the main altar. The noise and glitter of it held me spell-bound until it was over, but through it all I watched Mother and tried my best to do as she did. These visits had opened an entirely new and mysterious world that never left me. Every once in a while, later in my life, I found myself visiting or sitting in churches from little weather-beaten places of worship on the western prairies to the most imposing edifices in the United States and the vast cathedrals of Mexico. How much this may have been due to my going to church with Mother as a small boy in far away Silesia, or whether I did it unconsciously to still a strong pagan streak in me, I cannot say, but I do know that it always brings a certain peace of mind and reverence for life to me that no other experience can provide.

When I was well along in manhood, I often wondered how I had come by several of my individual

12

Christmas Eve

Left: Christmas scene in the Dayton church

traits of character and inclinations, such as my fondness for birds. I hadn't practiced art long before I somehow fell into etching and painting them in water color, and there are relatively few pieces I have written wherein their songs, flight, or being around, are not mentioned. They have been a part of my world since early boyhood, and I can truthfully say that awareness of birds was an inheritance from my paternal grandfather.

The old gentleman had always intrigued me, for he entered my life as a tall and imposing-looking man with a military bearing in his black frock coat, top hat, and cane. Being very proud of me, he frequently called on Mother to ask if he could take me for a walk in the city park to the fountain with its goldfishes, and, incidently [sic], to show me off to his cronies. From there we would head for his favorite "Weinstube" for a sociable drink, and I can still hear him instructing the waiter to bring me a glass with a little wine in it, add two lumps of sugar, and then fill it with fizz water.

For a man his age, he could still throw the ladies into a flutter whenever he turned up at social gatherings. Gossip had it that he had been quite a cavalier in his younger days, and, to add a final touch, a young lady of high degree had fallen so deeply in love with him that she was willing to give up everything to marry him. But Grandfather was a commoner and such a marriage was impossible, so nothing came of it. Eventually he found a petite golden-haired girl whom he married and who became my paternal grandmother. Their union was a happy one to its very end — which came suddenly. I well remember riding in an open *"fiacre"* with Father and Mother and poor old grief-stricken Grandfather in her funeral procession. About a month later Grandfather died, too — of a broken heart, his friends said.

However, the chief thing I remember him for was his love of birds. What else he did, I never heard mentioned, but when I knew him he always had plenty of spare time and spent it very much as he pleased.

In my time his great interest was in catching and raising wild songbirds — European varieties of redbreasts, thrushes, nightingales, and many others. Part of his home was filled with wooden cages of all sizes, and from them the din of song would come in almost deafening volume at certain times of the year. But it was the catching of birds that fascinated me the most, not because I liked to see them caught, but for the walks with Grandfather when he so painstakingly listened to their voices while tracking down some feathered little performer whose singing he especially liked. According to him, no two individu-

Chickadees waiting to be fed

als, even in the same species, sang alike, and it was quality in which he was most interested. Whenever he caught one that didn't satisfy him, he handled it with the tenderest of care while washing every trace of bird-lime from its plumage before turning it loose again. I spent many happy hours following him over fields, meadows, and through woodlands in his scouting expeditions for songbirds.

After Grandfather's death, my father had the best of the singers moved to our apartment in town, where an entire wall was hung with cages for several months. As melodious as their songs were, they could be ear-splitting at times, and they required daily care. So one warm spring day Mother and I hauled them, cages and all, to a strip of forest land along the river and turned the birds loose. The apartment seemed strangely quiet without them, but deep in my heart I was glad when we left them fluttering about in their native habitat.

During my years in Silesia I went through five grades of what would be considered grammar school in America. My greatest trouble from the beginning was to conform to regular class-room discipline, for up to that time I had pretty much followed my inclination toward whatever interested me most. I went through several periods of rebellion before I got straightened around.

I had learned to read quickly, which correspondingly widened my reading range at home, where I browsed in Greek Mythology, German Sagas, *Robinson Crusoe* and other romantic and juvenile literature that proved new and exciting to me. Nature was also claiming my interest. Wherever I went I came home with sacks full of branches, pinecones, flowers, etc. — also jars filled with beetles and butterflies, and one time a swollen face brought on by my deliberately prying into a hornet's nest.

Excessive reading diverted my attention from school and home studies. I had graduated to Jules Verne's works, books on exploration and discovery (mostly about North America), but above all I had run into the novels and tales by James Fennimore Cooper which, with my natural weakness for romance, fired my imagination as no other stories ever had. Mother, on a visit to Vienna, bought me a beautifully illustrated copy of *Leather-Stocking Tales* which I cherished more than any present she ever gave me. I read it from cover to cover, time and again, and felt sure that someday I would see the wild frontiers of that far country and perhaps have similar adventures myself. I doubt if any boy ever took Cooper's stories to heart more than I did.

The romantic literature wasn't all that threw my inner life into a turmoil at the time, for along with it

Mountain Chickadees

Blackbirds in a grain field

Courtesy Stuart and Kay Kleiber

H. Kleiber

Cedar Waxwings

Hans Kleiber

came my first love for a girl. There is no other sensation that can compare in purity to the first flush of a boy's admiration for a member of the opposite sex. It overwhelmed me so completely that I almost went out of my mind for fear of betraying my feelings. The object of my infatuation was a little blonde-brunette with dark grey eyes whom I sometimes met in company with an older sister on their way to a girls' school. The affair never went beyond shy glances and faint blushes and a few modest smiles, but it was enough to completely throw me out of gear. I was sure that if she spoke a single word to me, I would faint on the spot. When on stormy days the coachman drove the sisters to school or I somehow failed to get a glimpse of her, I felt as though nothing else in the world was worth living for. And so it went on until we left Silesia during the latter part of April 1900. But I never forgot that first love of mine.

I was just short of thirteen when my parents finally made the agonizing decision to leave their homeland. The thought of adventure won out over young love. I threw whatever weight I had in favor of a move to Leather Stocking country.

Upon arriving in the United States in May 1900, I

Disturbed

Left: Ducks rising from a marshy pond

21

had very little time to read any more classic prose or poetry. There were too many adjustments to make in coming to terms with the American way of life and picking up the English language.

Since my father was a textile designer, we, of necessity, settled in a small mill town in Massachusetts. What it offered disappointed me bitterly. While still in Europe I had read a good deal about America and expected to find a land of virgin forests, streams, plains, and mountains, with a few Indians thrown in. What actually greeted me were noisy factories, whistles, and smoke.

I entered the public school at once. There, strange to say, our first living quarters were in a French-Canadian neighborhood, and for months the school French I had acquired in the old country came in very handy while I played with the boys. It also proved a great help in my learning to speak English, for by the end of my first year I was able to make myself understood, although I must have mangled it rather amusingly now and then, judging from the way the boys parodied some of my expressions both in and out of school. That year was my last one of formal education.

When I was fourteen, sickness and other misfortunes overtook the family and made it necessary for me to find work to help support the household. I still read whenever I could, but it was mostly newspapers and magazines. I tried night high-school, but the subjects taught were such a disappointment to me that I decided to give it up.

For outdoor diversions I often took long hikes in the surrounding countryside or went on fishing trips with an uncle. I also played basketball on free nights and even became a star left-end on the local football team. I took up boxing, and that ended at an exhibition match with a semi-professional who, without knocking me out, gave me a clouting I long remembered.

I can think back on those early years in Massachusetts as a period of adjustment to a new land, but they in no way tarnished the luster of my early dreams and desires to see and live on the western frontiers. The books and magazines I read usually dealt with the out of doors. About 1904 I discovered some articles dealing with the forest reserves in the Far West and of the government's plan to establish a Forest Service some time in 1905. That immediately gave me ideas.

I became more restless day by day as I found myself falling into a groove which was claiming

Right: Chickadees

Hans Kleiber

23

Fish jumping for a fly

Left: Swallowtails

A rough stream

thousands of young striplings in our factory area. I had no intentions of following that pattern if I could help it. I had no fears of what might happen to me if I left home, but the family situation, as it was then, posed problems. It was difficult for me to arrive at any clear cut plan of what I ought to do.

The situation resolved itself in an entirely unexpected way. I had always been considered a fairly good draftsman and had often been told by teachers and others that I should do something about it. So when in the summer of 1905 I read an ad in the *New York World* about an artist in New York City wanting an apprentice in his studio, I sent him one of my drawings, and on the strength of that he asked me to come at once. My next problem was telling Mother, but much to my surprise she agreed it would be an opportunity worth following up and consented to my leaving.

After a few weeks with the New York artist, I concluded it wasn't what I wanted. In the meantime, however, I had met another artist who, sensing my predicament, very cordially invited me to live with him and his sister, who was a pianist, at their studio home near Fort Lee, New Jersey. My newly found friend wasn't so much an artist as a nature philosopher and a truly cultured American. I couldn't have been more fortunate for, besides teaching me something about the principles of art, he taught me the use of paint.

Of even more importance was the fact that he shared with me his very considerable knowledge of English and American literature. His high priests in the latter were Walt Whitman and Emerson and, from a philosophic standpoint, Henry David Thoreau. My friend came as near as any man I ever knew to living as Thoreau did in his cabin at Walden Pond. Where the latter kept a diary, Clarence Blodgett took his canvases and colors into the woods and fields to paint whatever happened to interest him. Along with this, his sister spared no time nor trouble in opening up the realms of music to me. I sometimes doubt if they realized the parts they so unassumingly played in Americanizing my education. My year with them was probably the most important epoch of my life in the United States and one for which I am everlastingly grateful.

Towards the last of my stay, my yearning to live in what remained of the western frontier asserted itself again. At the time, President Theodore Roosevelt was taking steps to set aside and protect forever the western forest lands that were left. I felt that unless I went now I would probably lose my last chance to have my boyhood dream come true. So I decided to forsake the arts for the present and go West to see

what part I could play in the President's plan for forests.

Young Hans was now ready to break the barrier that kept him from his first love. Forestry and all outdoors were so much a part of him that it could not be severed without maiming him. He must have realized that forestry and art are both such exacting professions that they could not be served at the same time.

When a man has so strong an inner drive, he does what he must. For Hans, it was now forestry. He could not possibly have known that this experience would one day give him a foundation for his art. Without that specialized background, he could not have penetrated so deeply into a world that few of us will ever see.

Hans Kleiber in the Wind River Mountains

Left: Autumn mountain scene

29

Mallard ducks rising

Doctor S. J. Wright collection

30

The strike

Hans Kleiber on the day he became a Ranger

PART TWO

HANS KLEIBER, FORESTER

Leaving the frontier

34

Hans Kleiber's first contact with the United States Forest Service was in Denver early in 1906. The Forest Service as we know it now was in the beginning stages of organization. Kleiber applied at the Denver office but found that he was too young to qualify for Civil Service jobs and was advised that the next best thing would be to work in a logging camp. Two areas were suggested to him — Flagstaff, Arizona, and Ranchester, Wyoming. Knowing nothing of either, Hans tossed a coin and it came up Ranchester, so he headed for the Big Horn country.

He liked the venture and the adventure from the start and found he had no trouble fitting into the life at the McShane Tie Camp at Woodrock. The men were cutting trees to be made into railroad ties for the Burlington Company, and Hans got experience in every phase of woods work.

In the summer of that year he did his first work for the Forest Service — marking timber at $3.00 per day. Kleiber and the Forest Service came to the Big Horn Mountains at about the same time, though Hans was not to become an official ranger for several years. He recalled that the first rangers' meeting in the Big Horns was held in 1906 at the Woodrock Station. In attendance were Gifford Pinchot, Overton Price, and Gene Bruce, an important lumberman from Washington, and the local personnel.

In the spring of 1908 Kleiber took his first ranger examination. It was held in the town of Big Horn, Wyoming, where the supervisor's office was then located. Applicants had been asked to bring their guns, as straight shooting seemed to be one of the requirements. Hans already held an appointment as Forest Guard, and he was told soon after the examination that he had passed. "On the strength of that," he wrote, "we all went out to celebrate; I was more pleased than I can tell." However, his elation was short-lived. Upon getting back to Woodrock sometime later, he found a letter from the Civil Service saying that in reviewing his application they had discovered that he was slightly underage and not a citizen of the United States. The last statement was a devastating blow; Kleiber had always thought his father had taken out final citizenship papers and that he and his sister were thereby made citizens, too, but it developed that the elder Kleiber had never completed the process. It was not until 1911 that Hans was able to obtain citizenship papers and get his appointment as a ranger.

Until the establishment of the district offices, the ranger station at Woodrock and the tie camp there seemed to be a favorite place for Washington officials and others to visit. Kleiber recalled a visit from Hamlin Garland, who had been sent by Gifford Pinchot to see the Forest Service at work and presumably to write a

Hans Kleiber: Forest Ranger on an inspection trip

book to publicize it. The resulting book, *Cavanaugh, the Forest Ranger*, was based on the Tensleep Cattle and Sheep War. Kleiber's opinion was that as a literary effort it was a "complete washout," adding little to the author's fame or that of the Forest Service.

Kleiber was not interested in the politics or the publicity of the Forest Service, either on the local or the national level, and to the end of his association with the organization he disliked this official "band wagon" phase of the work.

He liked best the assignments when he could deal directly with the things of nature. He was happiest exploring and mapping unknown areas, laying out trails, doing reconnaissance work, checking range conditions, and observing at close range the wild animals in their native lands or lakes.

By 1906 the white man, who had come to explore and to settle the Big Horn area, had driven the Indians from these prime hunting grounds. They had trapped and killed many of the wild animals and forced others to seek shelter in the high mountain canyons. During the years that followed, Hans Kleiber rode those mountains as a ranger and became familiar with the habits and habitats of the wild creatures that were left. Occasionally he made a survey and an official report on how many "predators" were probably in a given area, or investigated complaints by stockmen that coyotes and wolves, as well as bear, were raiding their herds.

But in his heart Hans saw these animals as individuals with feelings, hungers, fears, and passions much like those of mankind. He left one notebook full of stories about bears, his encounters with them and their struggle against the forces of nature, but, strangely enough, no etching was made of a bear. The following story relates his first encounter with a bear and also gives a vivid picture of his camp. He was to spend many happy, though sometimes lonely, nights in just such a "home"

Elk in the Rockies

Hans Kleiber

Doctor S. J. Wright collection

Along the Rockies

Left: Sheep, herder and wagon in the mountains

during the next two decades. At that time, it was a new experience for this young man from the East to be alone in a tent when night blanketed the Big Horns.

My First Bear Experience

I had just gone to work for the Forest Service, and I was camping by myself in order to be near my work. I had bought a twelve by fourteen foot tent and braced it with a frame work of lumber along its sides and roof and put a rough board floor under it to keep the moisture out. I was proud of it — my first home in the Big Horns. I furnished it with a small sheet iron cook-stove, a rough table covered with oil-cloth, a bunk with spruce boughs for a mattress, and a couple of stools. I built some shelves for my white enamel dishes and my food supplies. For tools I had two axes, one a double-bit, the other a timber cross-cut, and a shovel. For light I had a kerosene lantern and a dozen candles, as I always liked to read myself to sleep. I had placed the tent in a grove of young lodgepole pines into which I cut a clearing big enough to hold the tent and to give it shade and protection against wind and rain.

My job at the time was marking timber for the choppers and tie hacks. I had no sooner gotten started with my first day's work than some of the chopping crews told me of having seen a yearling black bear in the neighborhood of their camp, which was about a mile from mine. That very afternoon I saw the bear foraging in the willows not far above my tent, and I watched him for a while from sheer curiosity because it was the first one I had ever seen on the loose. Beyond that I gave him no further thought, as I had my supper to cook and was hungry from a day in the timber. I did, however, take my double-bitted axe to bed with me that night. I had not yet acquired a gun.

Being a light sleeper by nature, I was awakened by a scratching at the side of the tent closest to the frame brace, on which I had hung a slab of bacon. By the time my wits were functioning, the entire tent was rocking, and I felt as though the whole thing might fall down on top of me. I knew it was the black bear.

My first impulse was to reach for the double-bitted axe lying on the bed beside me, but on second thought decided that if I went to hacking at the side of the tent I would cut gashes in the canvas and ruin it beyond repair. Then I remembered my dishpan, into which I had put all my cooking pans, plates, cups, knives, forks, and spoons. Raising up as quietly as I could, I took the dishpan in both hands and flung it at the spot where the bear was trying to break in. The dishpan, with all that was in it, hit the spot with a

Camping

41

Camping in Upper Dinwoodie Canyon

clatter such as the bear, I am sure, had never heard before. Then I heard a mixture of loud snorts and snuffles as he tried his best to get away. In doing so, he must have become tangled up in the brush I had piled as I made the clearing for my tent, and for a few moments I didn't know what would happen next.

I fished around in the dark until I found my axe and stationed myself near the spot he had tried to get in — just in case he should change his mind about leaving. But he didn't even look back. Once free of the brush pile, he headed for the tall timber, snuffling and snorting as he went.

For some time after that, even a mouse rummaging around in my grub box would awaken me from my sleep, but the bruin never returned.

Much later in his career, and after Kleiber had become a self-taught expert on the habits of wild animals, he recorded another encounter. It reveals his empathy and understanding of the animals. In sparsely populated mountain areas, a particular bear or a particular wolf often became so well known to the men who lived there that he was a character to be talked about, even named and secretly admired. Men sought to outwit him, and the mountain grapevine carried reports of people seeing the animal, finding his trail and losing it again, and describing any peculiarity of this animal's physical make-up or his actions.

The legend of one such bear is recorded by Hans in a story he called "Mr. Cinnamon," and parts of it are quoted below:

One spring day a friend and I were crossing the head of Trap Canyon on Little Tongue River, when gusts of wind kept bringing sounds like the crying of a baby from somewhere in the brush. Both being mountain men, we knew at once that it came from a bear cub. We stopped and looked around, but in spite of the unobstructed view in the direction of where the voice came from we saw nothing.

We weren't particularly interested in meeting with a family of bear that morning, but few people can resist seeing or watching a small cub play around, especially when he cried as pathetically and persistently as this one. We looked the terrain over carefully again and again, but, not being able to catch sight of an old bear, we finally concluded that the little one might have strayed from his mother; we decided to hunt for him. He quit crying whenever we got near him, so it was some time before we found him — a brown cub about the size of a half-grown Collie pup. From past experience we well knew that the capturing of even a small cub can be a strenuous undertaking and had concluded that we should let him go. Just then the little fellow set up such a distressful racket, we couldn't abandon him. What to do with him after we caught him did not enter our heads.

We chased him up hill and down, over rocks, brush, and fallen timber until we were exhausted. Suddenly he dived under a couple of fallen trees. I had just gotten a good hold on the back of his neck when I noticed a black cub under there as well. We had no sooner gulped down that surprise when their mother, a good sized black bear, arose out of the dead branches at the other end.

No words can describe what we felt when that happened, for we had been caught red-handed kidnapping her babies. Neither one of us had a weapon, so we just stood there, literally frozen to the ground, staring at the mother and expecting inevitable retribution.

Within the moments that followed, I witnessed what was perhaps the most singular reaction I have ever known in an animal. Her eyes and whole attitude registered surprise, rather than anger, as she calmly took in the situation. She certainly did not reflect fear when to our unbounded astonishment, she settled down on her forelegs, began to whine for her cubs, then slowly, halting every few steps to see if they were following, she moved off.

Meanwhile, we retreated in the opposite direction, with as much grace and circumspection as we were capable of exercising, until we came to the foot of a solitary dead tree. We felt a lot safer there, for if she had changed her mind and decided to attack us, we certainly would have climbed it in a hurry.

Several days after the experience with the brown cub, I was working my way along the rim of the same canyon, about a mile farther down. Timber grew to the very edge of it, and I used the concealment it offered for the observing of any game which might be using the more or less bare south slopes and the canyon below. But most of all I had come to look for a brown bear with a slight limp in his right leg, whom I had seen occasionally and had heard of for over four years. He was a bear with an unusual history, most of which I was able to trace and piece together from events which actually happened and from items of range gossip as they were passed along by cowpunchers and sheepherders in the northern portion of the Big Horn Mountains. I doubt if anyone knew he was in Trap Canyon, and what had refreshed my interest in him was that I more than suspected he was the father of the brown cub we had tried to catch.

I was lucky that the wind blew toward me. Higher up, a spring gale was pushing a network of fleecy clouds over a very blue sky, and their shadows were beating up the full breadth of the canyon in

The Bighorns

The Absarokas, Wyoming

endless waves. Every now and then, the boulder-choked stream in the bottom, swollen from melting snows in the headwaters, tossed up a roar like distant thunder, so that, with the wind whistling around the cliffs and tearing through the trees, I had to depend on my eyes almost entirely to perceive what was going on around me.

I had come to a point jutting out from the rim and was standing in the shadows of a wind-twisted pine, from where an unusually extensive view could be had of the canyon, when I saw a brown bear lying on the sunny side of a big cliff, below and slightly ahead of me. He was close enough that I could tell he still had his winter coat, and, for having been out of hibernation only a short time, he was in good shape. Like most wild bear, he would get up frequently, walk and sniff the ground and bushes around him, test the air, and then lie down again. In doing this, I could see him favoring his right leg a little, which convinced me that he was the object of my search. One could tell he was at ease the way he stretched, scratched himself, and chewed at his shaggy fur. To run into him in such an unsuspecting mood was a find of the first order for me, and I settled myself to enjoy it as inconspicuously and quietly as possible.

I noticed that his attentions were focused on something down in, or across, the canyon. I followed

Maligne Lake

the general direction of his vision and discovered a black bear with a brown and a black cub prowling around the stream. I felt sure now that I was beholding the entire family within their home range, and that Mr. Cinnamon was the father of the brown cub we had tried so hard to catch.

Shortly after that, for no apparent reason, the big brown bear got up suddenly and walked around the cliff and disappeared. My seeing him had been a very lucky accident, and I had no desire to follow him farther, for my purpose of adding another link to my long acquaintance with him had been accomplished, and I was only too glad to have him go on living in peace.

The bears coming out of hibernation each spring found the mountains quiet and serene, moist from early rains. Trees grew, animals foraged, sparkling lakes were fed by melting snow, and a few hardy men rode horseback along the trails. Sheepherders jounced their canvas-topped wagons over rough terrain to get to summer pasture, and cattlemen brought their stock to the high verdant ranges.

Later in the season, the one great terror that could, and often did, disturb this calm was *fire*. Usually the fires were caused by lightning. A streak of light, a roar of thunder, and suddenly giant trees burst into flames as fire licked its way through dry timber and underbrush, sending wind-borne sparks miles away to start other devastating fires. Animals fleeing in front of the encroaching flames escaped or were burned to death if caught between two conflagrations.

As more people began to use the forests, the fire danger increased. There were fires caused by the carelessness of man as well as the lightning storms.

Spotting these fires and organizing crews to fight them became a major responsibility of the foresters. The urgency of quick action and the tremendous challenge of man pitting his skills and energies against this enemy of nature appealed to Kleiber. He said that being aware of how long it took a tree to grow and knowing how valuable it was to mankind gave him an incentive to throw all his energies into putting out a fire.

Although Hans had been working for the Forest Service as a guard for several years, he had gotten little experience in fire-fighting before 1910. That extremely hot, dry summer put the fire hazard at an all-time high, and, one after the other, fires broke out on the Big Horn Forest. One particularly bad fire was burning on the North Fork of Little Tongue and had burned over 2,000 acres. High winds fanned the flames fed by debris left on the forest floor after timber cutting. After working continuously for 48 hours on that fire, young Hans started to walk toward camp but fell exhausted by a big boulder and went to sleep. Some time later a large burnt

Winter on the range

Elk Lake — Bighorns

tree fell across the rock, but he escaped with only minor burns and injuries and limped on into camp. Later Kleiber was to become an expert on fire-fighting and was called upon to organize crews not only in Wyoming but also in Minnesota, Montana, and Idaho.

In 1913 Hans built the telephone line to Porcupine Ranger Station and one from Shell to Trapper Creek. He also rebuilt the line from Woodrock to Shell. This telephone communication system was a giant step forward in fire control because fires could be reported and crews dispatched speedily.

"Our old-time supervisor, Ed Jackson, had resigned and Cavanaugh took his place," wrote Kleiber in his notes. "He was long and strong on grazing control. One of the nerviest things Cavanaugh ever did was to hold a Government Roundup of cattle one summer on the Tongue District where there had been a good deal of trespassing. It was quite an occasion to see Forest Rangers playing cowboys. But it worked." About 1914 the Washington, D.C. office sent out men for "grazing reconnaissance." Kleiber liked this technical work and saw great possibilities in grazing as an economic policy for both ranchers and the Forest Service.

The oiled highway through Shell Canyon (U.S. 14) now makes traveling easy, safe, and scenic, as high-speed motor cars whisk tourists and natives from one side of the mountain to the other even in winter weather. It was not so in January 1915 when Hans Kleiber found it necessary to cross the Big Horn range from Dayton to Tensleep to take over a new assignment in the Paintrock and Tensleep area. His account of this winter trip and its hardships is memorable in contrast with transportation today and to remind us that Hans was one of the real pioneers of the Forest Service.

This was one of the toughest trips I ever made. I crossed the continental divide between Tongue and Shell Creek with a pack outfit on January 28th. Rangers McDonald and Anderson helped me up the east side and Ranger Weir down the west slope. I crossed just about where the highway is now. There were no roads then, and snow was stirrup-high the whole trip. A blizzard added to directional problems and made travel doubly difficult for me and for the horses. The trip from Dayton to Hyattville took four days. It was pitch dark long before I got to Hyattville, and, as there were no lights burning and no roads open, my only guide was the smell of burning cedar from some of the stoves in town. My overshoes were frozen to my stirrups, and Cavanaugh helped me alight from the saddle at the livery barn.

The next day, the Ranger who had resigned drove us by sled to the Longview Ranger Station, where we went over the district files and I took over the prop-

Across the Bighorn Divide,
January 26, 1915.

Across the Bighorn Divide, January 26, 1915

erty. We stayed there a couple of days and then went to Tensleep. The town was composed of a log post office, a log hotel, and a store. From there we drove by sled to the Tensleep Ranger Station. This was supposed to be the best equipped station on the Forest — and it was. In the living room was a good fireplace, before which I spent many comfortable, although lonely, evenings that winter.

Kleiber stayed there until May, when he was able to turn those assignments over to other rangers and accept an appointment back at Woodrock in the Tongue District with which he was more familiar.

Ranger Dickson and I cut the first wagon road through the timber, along which the highway now goes from Cutler Hill to Prune Creek. I had foreseen this as the most logical route toward Burgess for some time. Part of it had been used for old winter logging roads twenty years before that, but to open it up proved a considerable job. . . . I was also anxious to make that portion of the district accessible because it was all heavily timbered and seemed to be in the path of a lightning zone, and a number of such fires had occurred in there that had been difficult to combat.

The year 1918 was a bad one for fires. Kleiber had just moved his wife and two children and settled them at the Tanger Ranger Station for the summer when a call came that he was to report at Orofino, Idaho, where a fire raged on the Clearwater. "There was nothing to do but load the family on the buckboard again and haul them back to winter quarters at Dayton."

Kleiber found the Clearwater country pretty much

Right: Elk on the mountain

52

Hans Kleiber

Jack Reavis collection

Winter guests

Dayton, Wyoming

Winter guests II

enveloped by smoke from thirty-three lightning fires that had been started in one of the "finest Western White Pine Regions left in the United States." At the height of the fire he had 300 men in his camp, and all supplies had to be hauled 100 miles from the railroad.

"I was impressed by the size and quality of the timber and by the rainbow trout in Weitas Creek, a tributary of the Clearwater. I went out one morning after the fires were pretty well corraled and caught enough trout by noon to feed over 100 men all they could eat, and, to top it off, all those fish were caught with a willow pole."

Later he was summoned to northern Minnesota to direct operations on a particularly bad fire. This time he took his own fish pole, and, when the crew was hungry for something besides salt pork that had been shipped in by small boats and on pack horses, Kleiber caught enough northern pike and walleyes in one day to feed the crew of 200 men.

Fishing was one of his great joys, though seldom did he find occasion to do it on such a large scale as when he supplied food for the fire-fighting crews. "The Lone Fisherman" is one of Kleiber's most popular etchings, and those who knew him best feel this picture is a self-portrait of the artist in his most contented moments. The solitude and quiet of little mountain lakes had great appeal for Hans, and in them he found the peacefulness he craved. His etchings and his poems often portray his love for these remote lakes and streams. There he could dream his dreams, solve his problems, and store up in his heart that feeling of awe for natural things that was later to appear in his pictures.

The years weren't all forest fires, hazardous winter trips, or even solitary days. One assignment came to Hans that is humorous in retrospect but was perhaps more terrifying to him than facing a blizzard or a grizzly bear on a mountain trail.

He called the story "Red Light in the Forest."

A Forest Ranger is at times called on to perform duties which very few people think of as being part of his work. One of these calls came to me in the summer of 1909 while stationed at Woodrock, then headquarters of the McShane Timber Company, a large railroad tie and lumbering operation on the head of Tongue River in the Big Horns.

I was twenty-one at the time and was called into the office of the ranger in charge. After some preliminary spluttering, which was habitual with him whenever he had anything out of the ordinary to convey, he told me the Timber Company had lodged a complaint with the Forest Service that a "madam" from the Redlight District in Sheridan had set up a shop with three or four girls and several men com-

Night camp

panions, including a "tinhorn," in a park along the river a couple of miles below Woodrock. Their pursuits were interfering with the orderly conduct of the men working in the sawmill, and the Company felt it was the duty of the Forest Service to do something about it. "Old Rod" and I were assigned to investigate the charges and take whatever disciplinary action was necessary. It happened that I had just bought a new uniform, riding breeches, shirt and all. I slid into the outfit and pinned on my bronze badge. When "Old Rod" appeared, I noticed that he, too, had put on his best riding togs, besides having waxed his mustache, which he usually did if he thought the occasion demanded it. . . . .

We found the camp in a small, sheltered park almost completely surrounded by timber, with a stream close by . . . four or five tents, most of them new. Beside the road stood a big freight wagon with high side-boards in which they had brought their equipment and beds. Everything seemed to be set up in ship-shape.

With supper over and all the dishes cleared away, three gaily dressed girls, two of them young and pretty, sat on a log near a brightly burning fire, bantering a young man tuning up a guitar. A little apart sat an older woman, in her early forties I judged, and I took her to be the "madam." There were some extra

Fishing on Paint Rock

Fishing on Piney

The lone fisherman

horses tied to the pine saplings and a couple of cow-punchers, a sheepherder, and some lumberjacks were drifting in as Rod and I arrived.

We sent word by the teamster that we would like to talk to the "boss." She came to the edge of the clearing, where we stood red-faced and bumbling. She greeted us kindly but in a guarded manner as she observed our forest service uniforms, "What can I do for you two gentlemen this evening? Tie up your horses and stay awhile."

We told her about the Company complaints and our orders; I let Rod do most of the talking.

She listened attentively and after a pause replied, "I'm sorry to have caused the Company and you all this trouble. I just haven't been on a camping trip since I went on one with my father many years ago, and my girls have kept after me all summer long for a camp trip, so we just decided to take one." She pointed to the girls who were singing to the guitar accompaniment, "Do you see what a good time they are having? I have never seen them happier. It does them good to get away from their daily rounds in town."

The "madam" seemed to need to talk with someone, and the rangers were at hand. She talked at length about the kind of girls that worked for her, the different cir-cumstances that had sent them there, her efforts to help some of them and to solve the deep-seated problems that were covered up by a smiling exterior. "I do want my girls to be as happy as possible. An unhappy girl is no asset to any house."

She agreed to the request that their camp be moved off government property, and the rangers mounted their horses to ride back to the station — but not without a lingering glance at the merry crowd around the camp-fire.

Hans was a loner in many ways, but he was well liked by his legion of friends and his co-workers, and a good companion, as the following interview illustrates:

"Best winter I ever spent," commented Bill Hughey of Hiram, Utah, as he related the story of five months he and Hans spent together at the Windrock Ranger Station in 1913. Their job was to take snow cores each day and record the depth and moisture content of the samples. They rode horses or mules when possible, but if the snow was too deep for the animals the men traveled by snowshoes. "Hans never had a horse that wasn't also his friend. Whenever camp was made, care of the horses came first.

"We had dried food and staples," Mr. Hughey con-

Right: Winter scene

63

tinued, "and Hans kept us supplied with fresh fish, but we were getting mighty beef hungry until we found the calf. We came upon him one day standing in the willows, half frozen and looking lost. He had been missed when the roundup took all the other cattle out of the mountains for the winter. We butchered the calf and hung half of it in the meat house at the ranger station. The other half we made into corned beef.

"We figured that was our meat for the winter, but we almost lost it all. One day when we went to get a chunk out of the corning barrel, Hans pushed open the door to the meat house and saw something scooting around inside. A window hole two feet square let in enough light so we could see that it was a mountain lion. It had smelled fresh meat, crawled through the opening, and was ready for a feast. Hans grabbed his gun and pushed the door open with his foot. The big cat scrambled out between Hans's legs and knocked the gun out of his hand and into a three-foot snowbank."

Kleiber and Hughey stayed at the Windrock Ranger Station from November 27 to April 13. An early storm had blown the telephone line down, so they had no communication with the outside world during that time. For recreation, Mr. Hughey recalls that they had an old record player, went fishing, and in the evenings he played a guitar while Hans played his violin. He claimed that Kleiber was an accomplished violinist, a talent that the artist had never revealed to most of his friends.

A great many of Kleiber's etchings are of winter scenes. The stark, quiet cold of snow-covered mountains and meadows comes through forcefully in his pictures. He often combined this feel for winter with his great empathy for horses and drew pictures of these animals hunched up against a storm. He said once that he had a hard time learning to draw horses; their legs always looked like sticks, but he persisted and learned how to do it as he had learned most things — by himself.

His life was often fraught with danger, but Hans managed to survive perilous trips in subzero weather, burning trees, and encounters with hungry wild animals. He survived because he was knowledgeable.

Hans Kleiber was a good Forest Ranger, but he was much more than that. He was a biologist, a geologist, a conservationist, archeologist, an explorer, a humanitarian, and a rugged outdoorsman with the soul of an artist. He was an ecologist long before the nation became aware of its problems.

From 1906 to 1923, Kleiber worked for the United States Forest Service, and he did his work with unusual vigor, devotion, and understanding. He has left records of those years — terse government reports and personal notes. He chose poetry to express his feelings, impressions, and, often, his descriptive observations. Later he

Weathering a storm

Wintering in the Bighorns II

transferred those observations to pictures, and the greatest record left to us by this remarkable, versatile man is by Hans Kleiber, the artist.

To him the Forest Service was not just a job; it was a way of life. His relationship with the trees, the trails, the lakes, and the animals in the Big Horn Mountains was one of great emotional involvement. Unlike the average forester who thinks of trees in terms of timber, lumber, and ground cover, Kleiber saw them as living creatures and often endowed them with thoughts and philosophy.

I KNOW AN OLD WIND-TWISTED PINE*

I know an old wind-twisted pine
Up on a mesa top,
Where woodland birds, beginning spring,
In friendly gossip stop.

They come and go in pairs and flocks,
From travels far and wide,
And twitter in his limbs as though
They had much to confide.

I sometimes feel, between the two,
There is some hallowed bond,
And now and then they bring him news
From someone dear beyond.

It could well be, this someone dear
Had been a lovely maid,
Who vowed undying love to him
While lingering in his shade.

And that this vow of long ago
Is all that keeps him green,
And softly murmuring to the winds
Of things that might have been.

This fantasy and personification of trees may well have had its roots in the romantic stories and legends that he heard or read as a child in Austria. Many of his poems contain similar ideas.

His observations of animals are more realistic and seldom appear in his poetry. These he chose to portray in pictures. Two hundred thirty-nine of his etchings feature animals — a great majority of them are birds.

The realistic detail of the animals in Kleiber's pictures came from a close association with them in the forest. He relates one incident when this comradeship was almost closer than even an artist could wish:

I spotted an unusually large pool at the bend below me, framed by a grove of quaking aspens. Between keeping my eyes on the stream and its banks which were dotted with beaver holes, an event overtook me that words fail me to describe. In bending my arm back to make a good cast, I felt the tip of my fishing rod striking something that, instinctively, I knew wasn't aspen, dead or living. Turning about to see what it could have been, I found it had hit the horns of the biggest bull moose I had ever laid

*Hans Kleiber, *Songs of Wyoming* (Sheridan, Wyo.: The Mills Company, 1963), p. 92.

eyes on. He was standing as still as a statue within a few feet of me. One glance told me that his squinting little eyes were boding me no good and that the hackles along his neck were on the rise. The next thing I remember was hitting the deepest part of the hole, plunging through ice-cold water, waist deep, heading for the opposite side, and then clawing my way up a steep bank of gravel fifty feet or more high.

I never looked back until I had reached the timber on top of it. Stopping for a moment to gather my wits and catch my breath, I saw the old bull still standing where I had left him, but acting as though he wondered what had become of his intruder. Being fairly well acquainted with their inborn stupidity, poor eyesight, truculence, and other unpredictable traits of moose in general, I took no chances and headed upstream as noiselessly as possible. When I stopped to rest and to dismantle my fishing rod, it occurred to me that I had seen moose signs in several places below the slide, but with my mind so bent on fishing I had never dreamed of colliding with so huge a specimen. Ordinarily I should have smelled him at such close range.

Words may have failed Mr. Kleiber, but his paintbrush and his stylus certainly did not. In fine, significant lines he later etched into a copper plate the picture that was to become one of his most popular ones. He entitled it "Moose Moonlight." Others were called "Moose Swimming," "A Cow Moose and Calf," and "Returning from the Hunt." Fourteen of his etchings have moose in them. At least two fine large watercolors feature this animal.

Kleiber's scientific knowledge and keen detailed observations, as well as his reactions to nature, formed the background for much of his later artwork. "What you have never felt, you can't remember,"* and therein lay the strength of the associations between Kleiber's forestry days and his sensitive, delicate etchings and paintings. He did "feel" the majesty of forest animals, of birds in flight, of rock cliffs and trees.

"A poet," it has been said, "makes a tree, or a rock, or a mountain, an extension of himself, at least in the aesthetic sense."*

Hans the poet (or was it Hans the lonely man?) continued to find a fanciful companionship with trees. In his daydreaming he endowed them with human characteristics, and with them he developed a philosophy of life that blended man and nature. A piece of prose in one of his notebooks tells the story of a "conversation" with a tree. Scientific observer that he was, Hans began that story with a description of the trees that surrounded the

---

*Peggy Simson Curry, lecture at meeting of Wyoming Council on the Arts, Casper, 1971.

Lone moose

A pair of chickadees

Right: Mallard lighting

Courtesy Stuart and Kay Kleiber

Wintering elk

First Federal Savings and Loan Association, Sheridan, Wyoming

Returning from the hunt

Mallard ducks coming in for a landing

The Big Horns

setting of Horseshoe Springs. He described every specie of tree that grew in the "horseshoe" and told why, ecologically, each grew where it did — the tall dark spruce grew nearest the spring, the pines and aspens outlined the pattern and served as windbreaks for the taller trees. His "stories" are primarily nature lessons, but fanciful, interesting ideas are intertwined, as in the following bit of conversation between the man and a very old, large lodgepole pine tree with its "scaly, orange-colored trunk, twisted branches and crown."

"Doesn't it get monotonous being anchored to one spot and having to put up with the same neighbors and surroundings for seasons on end?" asked the man.

"I thought you would bring that up," the tree cheerfully replied. "It's something most animals, including man, cannot understand. We do not envy you in the least for being able to move around; this one trait of yours alone must pose no end of problems for you — and picture, if you can, what the world would be like if great forests of us began moving about."

The areas assigned to Hans by the Forest Service were extensive and mountainous. As a ranger he traversed them by horseback, inspecting the land and the trees, mediating the troubles that arose between stockmen and others, and, in the summer, fighting fire. There was little time for homelife, and Hans felt great conflict in trying to be fair to his family in Dayton and still give adequate time to his extensive and demanding job as a government ranger. One story that Kleiber wrote is poignantly autobiographical, with his own personal problems thinly disguised by transferring them to a family of squirrels.

The domestic life of Mr. and Mrs. Fremont, the squirrels, was constantly in turmoil because Mr. Fremont had to be away from the home tree so much as he gathered pine nuts and mushrooms for winter. Mrs. Fremont was afraid of coyotes and barking dogs, though she tried to forget her loneliness by taking care of the children and "listening to the chickadees as they cheeped away and looked under every scale in the bark of the tree for bugs and worms." Her thoughts drifted back to her husband, "He has always been a dreamer, and when those spells come on, it's hard for me to understand him. Whatever it may be, it's no fun to be left alone like this, and, for all I can tell, he may be up to something."

And the author of that story was indeed a dreamer; he spent long hours in quiet introspection. Gay and good company most of the time, but periodically given to hours of silence, Hans was an enigma to those closest to him. "Moody spells," said the people who were annoyed; "creative concentration" said those who were more understanding of his artistic nature. Perhaps this was why Kleiber loved his long days, alone on quiet

In the Rockies

78

mountain trails, camping on the shores of Lake Solitude, or silently observing a herd of elk in winter pasture. During these times he could be silent for hours on end and no one minded. Most of his poems "came upon" him during these quiet days, too, and he would pause to write down the words that flowed from his heart.

WHY DID WE MEET SO SOON TO PART*
Why did we meet so soon to part,
Why were our days so brief,
Yet in their briefness bring my heart
So much despair and grief?. . .

I never dreamed how deeply fraught
With love a heart could be,
But hardest comes to bear the thought
You were not meant for me.

In this world that was a strange mixture of reality and fantasy, Kleiber blended his responsibilities of checking on sheepherders and organizing fire-fighting crews, with philosophical thoughts, poetry, and his constant companion, an "Elfin Dame." Call it conscience; call it guiding spirit; call it what you will, but Hans called her his Elfin Dame.

---

*Songs, p. 88.

Left: Snow geese

SINCE MY DAYS OF CHILDHOOD MAGIC*
Since my days of childhood magic
An elfin dame whom none have seen
Has held my hand and guided me
As gently as a fairy queen.

When joy and laughter filled my days,
I heard her silver voice on high,
And when young griefs beset my heart,
I always found her standing by.

She walked with me and taught me how
Among the summer blooms to dream,
To listen to the lisping leaves
And catch the music of a stream.

When I was grown, she said one day,
"My lad, the time has come to roam.
This world is wide, your life is brief,
And all cannot be lived at home."

When love with all its torment came,
She whispered to me knowingly,
"Why don't you woo that lovely maid?
She sighs for you, her heart is free."

I wooed that maid, and others, too.
I loved to purpose, and in vain,
And when the dizzy round was done,
She took me by the hand again.

And like a child, I've never ceased,
Through all my sometimes stormy years,
To share with her, without reserve,
My loves and pleasures, and my tears.

---

*Songs, p. 63.

79

A shaded pool

Coming in

In 1920 Kleiber was designated as a ranger-at-large, in charge of range appraisal, mapping of fire lookouts, timber sale appraisals, relocation of old trails, and building of new ones. He liked this work because he had a special interest in the technical side of forestry and was concerned with the influence of the forest and its uses on the social and economic fabric in the surrounding country. In many ways Hans was years ahead of his time, aware of the problems and values of natural things while most people were still seeing them only as a business proposition — an inexhaustible source of supply. Office work and administrative duties, Kleiber did only because he had to.

On his new assignment Hans explored the Washakie and the Wind River country. He was asked to represent the Forest Service on an expedition that the Chamber of Commerce of Lander, Wyoming, was sponsoring for a party of "bigwigs" who wanted to explore the Wind River glaciers. "While ostensibly I was supposed to be an invited guest, it turned out that most of the work fell on me. There were thirty-odd saddle and pack horses in the party; the confusion was something to dream about." In spite of the long, grueling days and the difficulty of leading men who were completely unfamiliar with mountain climbing, Hans got them all up the mountain and back again without mishap and somehow found time to keep a detailed journal of every bit of flora

Snow in the Rockies

Elk in winter

Cloud Peak and Lake Solitude — 1933

and fauna as well as rock and glacier formations observed. "Parts of my diary on that trip were later published in *American Forests*."

Hans Kleiber was an explorer at heart, and some of his most exciting assignments and days in the Forest Service were those he spent blazing new trails, discovering unknown lakes, and climbing heretofore unclimbed mountain peaks. On July 23, 1922, Hans and a companion, Floyd Stalnaker, climbed Gannett Peak. He describes the trip and the mountain in typical official report style:

After crossing South Glacier, we went around a spur and ascended a prominent, steep, and very long snow couloir back of a pinnacle. Hard time here. Floyd most exhausted picking steps. Then took to rocks before getting to top, and had some good rock climbing for about 200 feet.... Found top of Gannett to be a fine edge with narrow jagged rocks, sheer precipice 2,500 feet to west. Glacier on east, and steep snow slope to edge of cliffs. Climbing on ridge sensational, quite like Victoria Ridge in Canadian Rockies. Top a mass of rocks with a good-sized topmost one on which Floyd and I could just stand. No record of previous ascent. Left our names in small friction-top tin under a monument which we erected. North and northeast of top is a snow dome.

Magnificent all-round view. We could see north to Yellowstone country. Many mountains in the east — Owl Creek and other ranges, also the plains. Southward, peak after peak of the Wind River Range — the big fellows. In the southwest, Fremont Lake and the town of Pinedale. In the west, the Gros Ventre Mountains and the long line of Tetons very sharp and clear.

Kleiber, the forester, recorded these detailed features of the Big Horns and surrounding mountains in his mind's eye and in his notes. Impressed and moved as he was by the magnificence of mountains, it is not surprising that so many of his etchings are dominated by mountain scenery. So forceful are the spare etched lines in his work that the strength and grandeur of mountains are conveyed to those who view his pictures.

On a trip to Bull Lake glaciers, he particularly observed ducks and other birds that appear so often in his etchings.

We put up a great many mallard and teal, and I judge that they raise their young in those marshes. The tall grasses and willow thickets certainly provide ample concealment, and topography here protects them from the intrusions of man, but raids from fox, marten, and hawks must be frequent, if the

Above: On Fremont Glacier, 1922 — Hans Kleiber on the right

Left: Gannett Peak from Elsie Pass, 1922

feathers and other remains could be taken as evidence.

Kleiber's notes on his exploration of the Wind River glaciers are a diary of starting times, miles traveled, obstacles encountered, and statistics that were of inestimable value to map makers, to other mountain climbers, and perhaps to hunters and prospectors. Following are some excerpts from those reports that may be of general interest and will also reinforce our image of Kleiber as a rugged outdoorsman and a scholar interested in every facet of learning and recording information.

In the Rocky Mountains, from their first uplift in the Western Plains to the shores of the Pacific, lie many regions on which Nature in her capricious moods bestowed much grandeur and beauty. Most of them have been thoroughly explored . . . and have become more or less accessible to the general public by roads or trails.

Here and there, however, are extensive areas that remain practically unknown to the sightseer. They are either a long distance from the beaten paths of travel or their topography is forbidding enough to hold off all but the most venturesome. One of these regions is found in the Wind River Range within the

The Tetons

Washakie and Bridger National Forests in the west central part of Wyoming. It is one of the highest and most inaccessible ranges of the Rocky Mountain system, and its crest for nearly 100 miles seldom drops below 11,000 feet elevation. Many of its peaks reach well above 13,000 feet. The highest of these is Mount Gannett, rearing its ice-capped summit for 13,785 feet into the heavens. Fremont Peak is the next highest and the most famous one, having been named for General John C. Fremont, intrepid explorer of the early West, who climbed it from the Green River slopes on August 15, 1842. Fremont's diary for this trip is detailed and precise. The description of the wilderness as an "unspeakable confusion of peaks and chasms into which the backbone of this range has been rent" is simple and one of the best that could be given.

The most curious statement that Fremont makes is that while the party was on the summit, surrounded by the absolute silence and solitude peculiar to such high elevations on still days, they observed the antics of a wandering bumble-bee. The veracity of this has often been questioned, but I am able to record from my own experiences that the ventures of these insects into high altitudes is truly remarkable. I have on a number of occasions found them buzzing among the last vestiges of plant life at elevations over 12,000 feet.

Scattered throughout Kleiber's notebooks are short articles on specific subjects showing his widespread interests and his tremendous store of self-taught facts. A concern for trees is evident, and they, too, were an important element in the watercolors and etchings that were to come.

Tree growth studies can add new dimensions of time to living things, especially as these are related to ourselves. I decided to take the time and trouble to count the life rings of a giant Englemann spruce which was cut by a logging operation. It was five feet in diameter at the stump and about 100 feet tall. I counted 800 rings — 800 years of life — and every log cut from that tree was sound. It was cut in the summer of 1909 and hauled by sleigh to a small flush pond just below the mouth of Prospect Creek the following winter.

Along with physical descriptions, Kleiber often inserted historical facts into his records: "Much of the Wind River country had been explored by Bonneville, Whitman, Fremont, Colter, and William P. Hunt.*

---

*Kleiber undoubtedly refers to Wilson Price Hunt.

Evening

Custer Battlefield

At Jackson Lake

91

Every season after 1849 brought its tide of emigrants sweeping along the south base of the Wind River Mountains. Great were the rendezvous when they met at the headwaters of the Green and Wind Rivers to barter their furs, exchange news, and indulge in such jollifications as the wilderness then offered."

A series of pioneer etchings later revealed Kleiber's respect for these hardy men and women who opened up the West. "An Indian Scout" is the drawing of Jim Baker, a well-known scout in the Rocky Mountain country about whom Kleiber had read in Cowbarth's *History of Wyoming*. This was one of the few portraits he drew. Others were of "An Old Plainsman," "Bill Cody," and an "Indian."

Among other pictures in the pioneer series were a fine one of Fort Laramie, several of the Deadwood Coach on the Bozeman Trail and covered wagons on the prairie, and some of the local saloons — the Bucket of Blood and the Last Chance. "A Prairie Burial" shows this artist's sensitive identification with the people who came before him. He had read of the incident in Francis Parkman's diary of 1846 and felt that it was so graphi-

Frontier days

Crossing the Platte

AN OLD PLAINSMAN

An old plainsman

Pioneers II

94

The trailherd

A burial on the prairie

The Bucket of Blood Saloon

Across the prairies

Evening on the trail

cally described in words by the author that he wanted to preserve the incident in picture.

In this group which included Indians, cowboys, pioneers, the Deadwood stage, an important fort, and the inevitable saloons, Hans gave a sampling of each phase of pioneering.

Though Hans speaks of the Bucket of Blood saloon as a "den of iniquity, still operating when I arrived in Sheridan," he speaks with much more feeling about a special little saloon in his home town and of the kindly, understanding man who owned it. As always, Kleiber chose poetry to express his deep feelings and emotional involvements. He explained in the introduction to his book of poems, *Songs of Wyoming*, that anyone reading them would find enough "biographical material to pretty well reveal the life of the man who wrote them and what made his clock tick." That is especially true in the following poem:

SOME THINK THAT BARKEEPS ARE ALL BAD*

I

Some think that Barkeeps are all bad,
But I, for one, must differ, lad.
It's been a trade with men of old
Since mead and wine were made and sold,
Any why men choose that way of life
Is no less strange than whom they wife.

_____
*Songs, p. 72-74.

For just as long as men drink beer,
The ones who sell it will be here:
Some are all right, and others not,
So why should we condemn the lot?

I never made a good bar-fly,
Though, now and then, I did get high.
For instance if some trifling wench
Had given my insides a wrench,
Or guy you told your troubles to
Betrayed your trust and told on you,
And then, across the friendly cup,
When things were on the up and up,

And you kept tossing down the stuff
When you well knew you'd had enough.

II

One time, when I was brash and young,
And caught on fortune's nether rung,
Deserted by my guiding star,
I stepped into the village bar:
In truth I had been sick so long
That I was feeling none too strong,
And walking in the blazing sun
Had sapped what little strength I'd won.

The place inside was dark and cool.
And sitting on a home-made stool,
A grey-haired barkeep, all alone,
Was listening to the gramophone.
His mustached face broke in a smile
That plainly said, "Sit down a while."
I thought it useless to disguise
My fix, and said, "A glass of beer —
A right nice place you've got in here."

"I'm glad you like it," he replied,
"I do my best." Then half aside,
"You know its easy to lose face,
When one conducts a drinking place."
He polished glasses for awhile,
Some idle moments to beguile,
Then said, "It's hot as hell today,
But that's all right for making hay."

By then I'd half drunk up my beer.
My courage rose, and with it cheer.
Yet, knowing not quite what to say,
I ventured in an offhand way,
"It's hot enough, I can agree,
But more than that is bothering me.
I guess Dame Luck just passed me by,
And left me feeling none too spry.
A bout with typhoid got me down
On Ruddy's ranch above your town —
Between us two, I'd gone so far
I saw the Pearly Gates ajar.

"I know it's tough to lie abed,"
He sort of low and thoughtful said,
"But things are never quite as bad
As what they sometimes seem, my lad:
The thing for you, I think the best
Is home-cooked grub, and plenty rest.

"It does no good to fret and stew,
I have in here a good old brew
I'm pretty sure will set you right,
And freshen up your appetite.
If it sounds queer, please do not laugh,
Among the trade, it's half-and-half.
A mix of English ale and stout
I do not need to brag about."

III

At first it tasted vile to me,
But soon I lapped it up like tea.
For weeks I drank six pints a day,
Or more to pass the time away.
Between I ate steaks by the score
And guzzled 'til the clothes I wore
Began to rip along the seams.
Some took this in with musing gleams,
But there were others not so kind,
Who loud and freely spoke their mind.
For one — up at the boarding house;
Its lady thought me quite a souse.

A life of Riley usually leaves
A taste behind that cloys and cleaves.
I had become a roisterous clown
Who'd gotten sick of life in town,
For idle weeks of food and drink
Had brought more hell than one would think.
But, really, what hurt me the most
Was parting from my barkeep host,
Whose kind advice would have been good
If I had used it as I should.
But being thoughtless, young, and gay,
I slipped the track and went astray.

When I stopped in to say good-bye,
He never asked the reason why
But took me out behind the place,
And pointing, said with sober face,
"You see those bins of empties there —
You drained of them more than your share!
If I were you, I'd cut it out."
With those few words, he turned about,
And with a knowing sort of wink,
He left me standing there, to think.

At the Silver Dollar

By his own clear thinking, Hans seems to have solved the problem.

A problem that could not be resolved was the relationship with his wife, Frances. She was an eastern girl and had never fully adapted to the rugged life of a pioneer Wyoming town or to the fact that his work kept her husband away from home most of the time. Nor could she understand his strange periods of silence. They had been married in Cambridge, Massachusetts, on April 11, 1911, and were divorced in 1919. Later, in reminiscing about his mother, Hans wrote, "She left her comfortable home in Massachusetts without a qualm, to take over my household in Wyoming. She practically raised my two children, and she and my invalid father lived with me in Dayton until they both died." At the time of the final divorce, Rita Louise was six years old and Stuart was five.

In spite of his introspection and his great absorption with the things of nature, Kleiber as a Forest Ranger met some interesting individuals in the course of his daily work. He liked this part of his job, too, and often wrote up the encounter either in a poem or a story. Humanitarian that he was, Kleiber took great personal interest in each one and felt a responsibility for the welfare of even the most unlikely characters if they were in the area under his jurisdiction.

There was Old Jake, hiding out from the law, who

The Kleiber Family, Dayton, Wyoming, about 1915

took a shot at Kleiber the first time they met and then laid down his rifle and asked if Hans would look over some of the poems he had written.

There were the sheepherders who shared mutton stew with him as he visited their remote mountain camps. Kleiber seemed to feel a kinship with these herders as they kept their lonely vigil months on end without human companionship. Several fine etchings and one of his Christmas cards reveal the artist's understanding and appreciation.

Then there were people like the old woman and her tiny shivering dog that he found one blizzardy day in an isolated cabin. The winter wind had blown the door off its hinges, and there were no panes in the windows. The winkled old woman wrapped in a ragged blanket sat hunched in front of a smoky, cast iron stove. She clutched the whimpering dog. As a ranger, it was Kleiber's duty to see to the welfare of any persons in his area, but his human sympathy and curiosity in this case far outweighed duty. He finally discerned from her few halting words that she had come up several days ago in a wagon with her son, who wanted to hunt. That morning he had gone out and not returned. Accustomed as he was to traveling mountain trails, the ranger still could not believe that a wagon had crossed the half-frozen creeks and traversed the rocky trail that led to the cabin, but the wagon was there, and so was the pitiful, frightened old woman. Hans made her as comfortable as possible and then went out to locate her son. This he did and checked to see that they got safely out of the rugged mountain area and onto a road toward their home on the east slope.

"Poetry, as a literary form of expression, has held me in its grip since my boyhood days," Kleiber wrote in the introduction to *Songs of Wyoming*. "I always felt there were so many incidents, personal reactions, and straying thoughts, or states of heart and mind that are next to impossible to render in a more telling way, that I often took refuge in it while following my career in the Forest Service and finally into the arts."*

He chose this mode of expression to tell the story of another interesting character he met in the course of his daily work assignments. The following ballad describes an incident at Woodrock in 1909. It is more than a story of one man's life and violent death. In it Hans reveals his compassion for mankind and its problems. As always, this author asks "Why?" and strives to understand the motivation behind man's actions. He also searches for a solution and in the last stanza offers a belief in God as the strength which will carry men through problems and tragedies.

A ballad meter and form are used, and Kleiber divides the poem into two sections — the first one relating the actions of "Old Pete" and of the men who buried him. The second part is reflective and philosophical. He consistently used a rhyme scheme of ABCBDB, and in most stanzas the fifth line has an internal rhyme.

Old Pete*

The bunkhouse door burst open wide,
And from the night, half-clad,
A wild-eyed jack rushed in and screamed,
"Old Pete must have gone mad.
He chopped his hand off at the wrist,
And boys, it sure looks bad!"

Songs, pp. xii-xiii.
Songs, pp. 37-40.

When we got to his lonely shack
The time of help was by,
And seeing Pete lie in his blood
A man let out a cry:
"Lord, what a sight by lantern light,
And what a way to die!"

Some wondered what abysmal griefs
Or fears his soul had nursed
That called for such a frightful deed;
And there were those that cursed,
But most just stood, like men of wood,
And speak would scarcely durst.

In lumber camps, far in the woods,
Men only seldom choose
To snuff their lives for past regrets,
They can afford to lose;
For blood does glow, so red in snow,
If one will stop to muse.

We laid him in a rough pine box
With little thought of show,
Then covered him with green spruce bough
To hide its load of woe;
While magpies fought for every clot,
Outside, upon the snow.

We worked next day and most the night
With little said in mirth;
For many a load of wood it took
To thaw that frozen berth
Full five feet deep, so Pete could sleep
In peace in Mother Earth.

The bitter cold went to our bones,
And heard was not a sound,
Except the squeaking of the sled,
As down the trail we wound,
To offer mute, our last tribute,
And lay Pete in the ground.

Each man had given more than cash
To lay his corpse away.
No tears were shed, nor rituals read,
For none knew what to say.
But each one wished Godspeed to Pete,
And in his heart did pray.

II

What brought Pete here was known to few.
Most hands thought him a freak
Who worked apart and lived alone
And did not friendship seek;
Not until booze his tongue would loose,
With burning eyes he'd speak.

It was a tale that through his life
Had rent a ragged seam.
A wife, a home, and happiness,
And then a scorching gleam,
How she had strayed and then betrayed
Him in his blissful dream.

Some try to mend the broken shards;
Some laugh, and others cry.
And some will kill when love goes wrong
With steady fateful eye.
But like a deer, Pete fled with fear
Into the woods to die.

Of little worth are earthly goods,
Or kindling of remorse
In stricken hearts that stumbled on
Their blind haphazard course,
When they have lagged and slowly dragged
Themselves from bad to worse.

To still the specter in his mind,
Pete sought from whiskey aid,
But found its cup of no avail;
And fancy girls who played
With him for gold would leave him cold
And only deeper frayed.

Then he would seek the woods again,
All by himself to wring
Some compromise from ugly fate
To stop that hideous thing
From running rife, which to his life,
But hell on earth could bring.

Try as Pete would, he never could
Deny himself a drink,
Until at last it crazed his mind
And brought him to the brink,
A sodden clod who'd lost his God
And could no deeper sink.

That winter night, in his lone shack,
He paid his final toll.
Perhaps, at last, fate spun so fast
Despair engulfed his soul,
And made it but a little step
For him to cross the goal.

Maligne Lake I

Right: Big Horn Sheep in the mountains

106

H. Kleiber

Fremont Peak, WindRiver Mts

107

Old Pete has lain for many years
Within his woodland grave.
The Chickadees above him cheep,
And harebells gently wave.
But I still think, how on its brink,
That cold, grim winter day
We for his soul did pray.

To those who carry riven hearts
And life is all travail,
An all abiding faith in God
Will never let you fail.
However great and deep the loss,
Your soul to save, HIS SON He gave
To die upon the cross.

Hans Kleiber, the compassionate man, is revealed in his poems.

During the latter part of 1922 Kleiber had been given a major assignment of examining and evaluating the grazing resources of the Wind River Range. It was a time of mapping and recording, but it was also a time of soul-searching for Hans. The spread of glinting peaks and valleys in this mountain range cast an awesome spell on the potential artist. "With all this vastness surrounding me, I began to wonder if it really were within a man's power to give an adequate expression of such things in paint. The more I thought about it, the more I began to doubt my own untried abilities in that direction. In early sporadic efforts undertaken so far, I had found that it is one thing to be moved by strong feelings and quite another to put them into execution. And yet, I wanted to try it more than anything else that I had ever wanted to do in my life." As he climed down from Wiggins Peak on the West Fork of the Wind River, the thought would not leave him, and it was on that day that Hans Kleiber determined he would resign from the Forest Service as soon as this assignment was concluded and take a try at art.

Still watching the sun set behind the far-off Tetons, Hans saw first one mountain sheep and then another come out of a patch of stunted spruce along the rim of Caldwell Canyon below him until fourteen of them were grazing on the sparse vegetation between the rocks. From memory that scene was to be etched on copper plates and painted on canvas.

A sudden storm on the mountain, and that night spent in a soaked bedroll, confirmed Kleiber's decision to change his vocation. He instinctively protected his hands from the bitter cold as he peered out of his tent the next morning upon a world blanketed with snow.

"I had gone into forestry for the pure love of it," wrote Hans in one of his papers. "My years of work for the Service filled a niche in my life that nothing else could have filled with deeper satisfaction and enjoyment. The work itself and the money I got for it, while important enough in their way, had always been of secondary consideration. It had been a way of life for me."

It was not easy for Hans to turn his back on this and

In the Big Horns

109

Sheepherder's farewell

take up an entirely new way of life, but since "about 1920" he had been thinking seriously of turning to art as a full-time profession. "The inner urge became stronger as time went on, and finally I knew that if I didn't do something about it soon, I probably never would. Manual processes and a complete turn about in modes of living are harder to make after a man has passed his thirty-five year mark, and I had recently reached that milestone."

Even though he had done little in the line of art since those few lessons in New York in 1905, the roots were there, and a longing for it kept cropping up more and more insistently as the years went by. "I wanted to express in pictures some of the things I had seen and felt."

Kleiber wasn't at all sure he could succeed in this purely creative endeavor; he knew he had two children and his parents to support, but he also knew he had to try. He resigned from the Forest Service early in 1923. "I didn't do it to get a better job or earn more money. Art is a far more exacting and jealous mistress than forestry, and those whom she has called have little chance to escape."

The following letter taken from the files of the Forest Service is an official recognition of the unusual loyalty that Hans Kleiber displayed in his work with that organization.

UNITED STATES DEPARTMENT OF AGRICULTURE
FOREST SERVICE
ROCKY MOUNTAIN DISTRICT

Federal Building
Denver, Colorado
May 10, 1924

Mr. H. N. Kleiber
Dayton, Wyoming

Dear Kleiber:

I am sure you will be interested in the following comment from the inspection report made by Forest Inspector Kelley of the Washington Office, who visited your fire camp on the Superior last spring:

"In closing this chapter I want to say that perhaps former ranger Kleiber of the Washakie exhibited typical District 2 spirit on the Superior last season. His resignation had been accepted by the Supervisor but was unknown to the District Forester. A telegram was sent by the District Forester asking Kleiber to report for fire duty on the Superior. The Supervisor put it up to him. He never hesitated. 'Sure I'll go!'

"He went — out to a remote section of the 97 fire, where, for more than a week without aid or even receiving an encouraging word from the District Ranger, he searched out and learned the topography, located the lead of the fire, organized the crew as best he could under the circumstances, and directed the fight — not from camp, but out on the line. He was not discouraged nor daunted by the neglect of local officers nor by the broadside, lump-developing, blood-sucking onslaught of black flies and mosquitoes.

"This case was one of the most striking examples of devotion to the Service and to the cause of forestry that it has ever been my fortune to encounter."

Very sincerely yours,

C. M. Granger
Assistant District Forester

Hans was never a man to do things by halves. He knew that he could not serve two masters and that upon leaving the Forest Service his old freedom to roam the mountains was over.

FAREWELL, MY OWN BIG HORNS, FAREWELL*

Farewell, my own Big Horns, farewell!
You lie so white and still,
While in me sounds a parting knell
And tears my vision fill.

Why could not your towering crest
A storm have hid this day?
Instead you charm me at your best
When I must go away.

Your snowbound peaks like diadems
Are glittering in the sky.
Why do you thus blaze in your gems
When I must say good-bye?

The valleys basking at your feet
Are budding green and fair;
Spring never gave a day more sweet
Or gentler stirred the air.

Farewell, again, you white-robed slopes!
May fortune never spurn
Within my heart the ardent hopes
That bid me to return.

Winter in the Bighorns, 1939

―――――
*Songs, pp. 4-5.

PART THREE

HANS KLEIBER, ARTIST

Hans Kleiber traveled a long, hard road to artistic integrity. Rarely have a man's life and his art been so interrelated, and this closeness is best interpreted by his own writing and poetry and by excerpts from a revealing business correspondence.

Old-timers have filled in some gaps. Because Blanch Clapham had the forethought to bring us together, we have Bill Hughey's vivid account of the five months he spent with Hans, snowed-in in the high country, an experience that later resulted in many etchings.

From Harry and Margaret Fulmer we have the story of Hans and Missie Kleiber's wedding in 1931. The reception was held at the Fulmer ranch home. The already lively party developed even more action when the curtains caught fire. The blaze was extinguished by guests who were accustomed to dealing on their own with unexpected situations.

Outstanding help was also given by 91-year-old Arthur Dickson, Hans's neighbor in Dayton, Wyoming. "Hans was shorter than tall and had big, strong hands," commented Dickson as his description made Hans come alive for us. "He was all man and far from an

Left: Hans Kleiber on the front porch of his studio in Dayton, Wyoming, 1965.

uncomplicated one. Like most artists, he must have had inner doubts and complexities, but he resolved those during long spells of thinking in private."

What his friends saw was a man of sturdy build and a pair of eyes that no one ever forgot. They were intensely blue and gave the feeling that there was not much in man or nature that escaped him. They also mirrored his own feelings, and their expression was usually humorous and always warm with feeling.

Emmie Mygatt uses the personal pronoun in this section of the book because it covers twenty-five years of close friendship with Hans and his fun-loving, lively Missy. Emmie and her husband, Ken, shared many happy hours with those two, in the mountains, in their respective homes, and in Hans's studio.

The Mygatts were even privileged to visit Mrs. Tarbox's woodshed. Mrs. Tarbox was Hans's mother-in-law. He used to tell us that, just as a writer needs a big wastebasket, so an artist must have a place to file his mistakes. He took delight in papering the woodshed with his discards and allowed special friends to look them over. A layman might not notice imperfections, but Hans's self-criticism was wise, realistic, and unsparing.

We did not know Hans until 1936, but I have often wondered what went on behind those deep blue eyes as Hans sat on Wiggins Peak and made his final decision to leave forestry for a career in art. I don't suppose he thought anything as precise as — This I have seen — This I have lived — This talent I have — And this I must now pass on to others. But, in effect, that is what he must have done. Consciously or unconsciously he would pour his knowledge, love, and the tranquility of unspoiled nature into his pictures.

How does a bird sitting on a mountaintop suddenly decide in which direction to fly? He doesn't. He is impelled by natural forces that have been guiding him since birth. So it was with Hans. His decision to leave forestry and live with art was no sudden thing. It came from an instinct born in him which grew throughout years of thinking, planning, learning, dreaming, and enjoying what he was doing, but slowly realizing that forestry was actually a preparation for work to come.

What a responsible person thinks at such a time would differ radically from the thoughts of an irresponsible one. Hans owned a house in Dayton and had enough money saved to carry his family for two years. But what if he did not succeed in two years? Dare he subject his dependents to the risks and uncertainties of so radical a change in profession? He was thirty-five; if he waited much longer, he might not be able to make the change. Could he transfer his love and knowledge of the mountains and its animals from direct contact to the abstraction of art?

In 1923 Hans was not yet married to Margaret Duff, and his former wife, Frances, had remarried. So at this time his family responsibilities consisted of two children, Rita and Stuart, and his own parents. From his earliest days Hans always spoke of his father as a man of stature, and so he was. But until we visited with Arthur Dickson and then found a family picture, we had never realized that the elder Mr. Kleiber was quite lame and hunched over, and was by this time an invalid. Hans could not fail this little group. How he tackled the problems of his new career is best told by the artist himself.

"My first efforts to gain a foothold in the arts proved to be a bootstrap-lifting operation because I had no capital to finance even the elementary training necessary to acquire the manual processes of different mediums. Aside from that, and to make things still tougher, I had made up my mind not to go in for the commercial end of it, which is chosen by so many artists as a way to stay solvent. Finally, I had a family to support.

"Taken altogether, these choices and obligations proved rather hard to abide by, because I soon discovered that there was far more to art than I had supposed. The hardest part was to find out what I was best fitted for, how to express what I saw and felt in a medium congenial to me. There were times when this became extremely confusing, so I finally began teaching myself

The log boom

My home town — Dayton, Wyoming

118

to draw in pencil and crayon and, later, in pen and ink. From the latter, as I had always liked prints, I decided to try etching. After no end of trials and errors, it being anything but a simple medium, I began to see possibilities and concentrated on mastering this form. From etching, I gradually drifted into water colors and also did a lot of sketching in oils. For years there was hardly a holiday excursion or pack trip that I didn't take a box of panels and papers with me. In whatever I do, Mother Nature remains the supreme teacher, and I am willing to leave abstractions and brainstorms to those who are inclined toward that side of art."

The actual mechanics of etching are unfamiliar to many people, and they are interesting in themselves. Hans became completely absorbed in mastering this medium, so much so that his periods of silence and reflection increased. Arthur Dickson says of these times, "You couldn't get a word out of him. Not everyone agreed, but I felt it was an inner searching. Hans needed time to reflect, and his introspective moods were creative."

Mr. Dickson continued, "I get expansive when I think of Hans; he added dimensions to people's lives — an endearing man and good company. Out of these silent times came hard-won, self-taught knowledge and decisions which Hans applied in a practical manner."

Hans was often asked where he went to art school to learn the manual process of etching. Actually, he never went to a class in it, but after this period of soul-searching he decided to experiment with etching and bought a small paperback book on etching and printing, published by Winsow and Newton in London, England. It cost two shillings. After "reading the book forward and backward," he bought the necessary supplies and went to work. It was a trial-and-error method of learning from the start. If the results didn't turn out as the instructions stated they should, he simply started all over again and kept at it until they did.

After etching a plate, his next big problem was to devise some way of printing it to see what it looked like on paper.

Since there were no printers of etchings anywhere in Wyoming, he rigged up a wash wringer with rubber rollers, but the results were totally inadequate. So he designed a press patterned after a picture in another booklet he had bought.

Hans made his first press with an iron bed and with gears and steel rollers cast by the Iron Works in Sheridan, Wyoming. These he bolted to a homemade wooden frame. That contraption, crude as it was, saw him through until after the first exhibition at Goodspeed's in Boston in 1928. From that exhibition he made enough money to order a medium-sized press from Kimbers in

Hans Kleiber

London, which he used for all the hundreds of prints that he was to make during his most productive years.

Many people think the difference between an etching and a pen-and-ink drawing is only a slight one. "Nothing could be a greater mistake," wrote Hans in his *Notes on Etching*," as the problems of etching are much more intricate and the final effect achieved by it is infinitely richer and more telling than any pen-and-ink drawing could possibly be." Etching challenges the highest abilities of the artist in design and execution and compares well in that respect with any effect that may be achieved in painting.

An etching is always engraved into a wax-covered metal plate and then printed on paper. Because this procedure reverses the image as drawn by the artist, he often sits with his back to the view he wants to sketch, looking into a mirror in front of him, where he sees everything sides exchanged. For engraving he uses a very sharp needle or a diamond-point needle; if he makes a mistake, the whole plate is spoiled. When the drawing on the metal plate is finished, the artist puts the wax-covered plate into an acid which eats the lines into the metal until the picture has the shades or tones he wants. He may have to repeat the process several times to achieve his desired effects.

Left: Winter ranch scene

In order to take an impression from the plate, the wax has to be removed and a stiff black ink rubbed into the lines by hand. All superfluous ink has to be taken off again by hand. Then the printer takes a wet sheet of paper, puts the plate on top of it, and wheels both the paper and the plate through a printing press. A plate cannot be used indefinitely; at most about a hundred prints can be taken from it. Each one of these prints is considered an original if it is signed by the artist.

Most artists, while learning their skills, have had museums accessible to them, where they may even set up an easel and work from a master's picture. Hans did not; he had to study books and reproductions. Among his favorites was Benson, whose work he copied while developing a style of his own. To quote Bertha Jaques, former secretary of the Chicago Society of Etchers, "His technique has been practically self-taught. There are no tricks; it is all honest work that does not change with the fads of the moment. . . . It will furnish a record of life in the West that is being altered by so-called civilization."

As a result of all this self-teaching, Hans was able to master the techniques of an art form which allowed him to portray his great understanding of the mountains. His etchings were eagerly bought throughout the Big Horn country. It was typical of the man that he made no effort to publicize his work more widely. This came about quite by accident. In 1923 Hans left the mountaintop and forestry after making his decision. In 1926 a Mr. Kettell, an eastern dude, visited Hans's studio. A connoisseur of prints, Mr. Kettell was so impressed by what he saw that he took Kleiber's etchings East with him to Goodspeed's in Boston, a well-known print and bookshop. Immediate correspondence resulted and was followed by a large showing in January 1928. Excerpts from the Goodspeed letters reveal much about a man now moving into artistic big time, not by his own pushing but by others' recognition of his merit.

The first letter, dated June 4, 1926, is typical of many which were to follow. It was written to Hans by Louis Holman of Goodspeed's Book Shop: "You express my own feelings perfectly when you say that the pleasure of having time to devote unreservedly to art has all the thrills that a boy experiences when circus time comes around. You will find a great satisfaction in opening up the beauties of the world, which to the great crowd are practically nonexistent."

October 24, 1927: Fifty prints would make a very comfortable showing in our gallery. We appreciate the difficulties under which you work getting prints from a homemade press. Your suggestion of $5 per print is rather a small price for an etching; we think yours should be priced somewhat above this, not exorbitantly but from $7.50 to $15.

December 3, 1927: Dates of exhibition have been set for January 3rd to 14th. We would like to take over complete distribution of Kleiber prints — both wholesale and retail — distributing prints to various dealers in the U.S. and to local markets in Boston.

May 2, 1928: Editor of *Sportsman* magazine offers to buy "Geese in Flight" and one or two others for their fall issue.

January 16, 1928, Charles Childs of Goodspeed's in Boston to Hans Kleiber: Exhibition has gone off well; enclosed is clipping from *Boston Transcript* of Jan. 7. We are sending several of your prints to England and to dealers in the U.S. Can you let us have duplicates of the bird prints immediately? It seems there will be good demand for them.

March 26, 1928: The new plates are very satisfactory, and we are much pleased with the quality of the aquatint work. There is very little good work being done in aquatint today, possibly because etching takes the popular fancy more quickly or possibly because of the difficulty in handling the medium in a way to get complete satisfaction. I hope you will do more plates in this medium and style.

April 25, 1928: The new aquatints and drypoints have arrived, and we are very much pleased with them. We shall have another check to send you in a few days.

Right: Kleiber at work in his studio, 1965

122

Kleiber – 1930

Leaving the high country

124

Cypress swamp

125

July 2, 1928: Your prints were represented in company with those of George C. Wales and Samuel Chamberlain at the exhibition in England.

February 1, 1928: We are glad that you are to have prints exhibited in the International Printmaker's Exhibition in Los Angeles. We shall do our best to keep your prints current . . . new ones are always welcome.

February 18, 1929: We telegraphed you today asking for additional prints of the colored plate "Mallards Disturbed." We need more of "Starting on the Hunt" and more of "Brant." We feel sure it would be to your advantage to make a number of colored prints, particularly if they turn out as well as "Mallards Disturbed." We are strong for the color plates.

January 7, 1930: I am glad you think it will be possible for you to come East this spring. . . . I can understand your hesitance about meeting people who are usually more curious than interested. One has to acquire a certain veneer of callousness to do it constantly without flinching. . . . Am sure you will find the exhibition pleasant rather than distressing. "Geese Crossing Wyoming" now seems to have greatest popular appeal . . . because of fine composition and the beautiful atmospheric quality. Eager sportsmen would welcome more of this kind. Send more of "A Flock Rising" (on creamy paper) and of "Teal."

The early Goodspeed letters show Hans's unin-

hibited joy in at last holding the tools of his art in his hands. How long he thought about doing this is revealed by entries in his Forest Ranger diaries, where he sometimes mentions the special care he gave his hands. In his first letter to Goodspeed, Hans compares himself to a small boy at a circus. Actually, he was more like a bridegroom who had courted his bride for many years and, having won her, is more in love than ever.

His first exhibition at Goodspeed's was followed by many others and by honors that sought him out. An early one, in 1929, was a silver medal awarded by the International Print Makers of California for his etching "Leaving the High Country."

Kleiber rarely left home to attend exhibitions — actually never, unless urgently summoned for some special occasion. His first trip was to a one-man show at Goodspeed's in Boston. If, during his most productive years, he had visited all his exhibitions, he would have had little time to paint or draw. Some were as close as Denver and Salt Lake City, but even these he did not attend. Nor did he go to most of the showings held in New York, throughout California, in the National Gallery in Washington, D.C., in New Orleans, throughout the Midwest and, of course, repeatedly in Boston. Nor did he go to the exhibition in London, England, or the International Art Exhibit in Italy.

World War II broke out during the International Art

Bayou Teche

127

Hans Kleiber at his studio press, 1965

The old homestead

exhibit in Venice, and Hans's work was not returned until the war was over. Getting it back was quite a problem; Hans's naturalization papers, acquired in 1912, had been mislaid, and he had to prove citizenship before the pictures could be returned.

Goodspeed's customers in Boston urged Hans to come to New England and live there for a time, long enough to study and to do a series on New England birds. He never found time for this, but he did go to Louisiana at the invitation of duck-hunting friends. They invited Kleiber to stay at their club and gave him a guide to the bird sanctuaries and bayous. He had a very happy time there, and a series of delightful pictures resulted.

So much for his worldly honors. In 1931 he married Margaret Duff, always known as Missy. Recently, when I picked up Rachel Carson's book *The Sense of Wonder*, I thought of those two. In her own individual way, Missy

Virginia deer

Canvas back

Pintail

Mallard

American Widgeon

Blue Winged Teal

Shoveller

Harlequin

Drakes

shared Hans's joy in living. On the bottom of Rachel Carson's book jacket it says, "Words and pictures to help you keep alive your child's inborn sense of wonder, and renew your own delight in the mysteries of earth, sea and sky." Hans was like that; he conveyed his own pleasure to others through pictures, and knowing the man makes one realize why he was able to do so.

Life went well for the Kleibers. Hans had more work planned than he could ever do, and he and Missy had more friends than they had time to see.

As his fame spread, curious visitors became a problem. To reach Hans's rustic studio with its old-fashioned press, they had to pass the Kleiber home. Often they were strangers, and Missy, knowing that Hans needed protection, jokingly referred to herself as a spider sitting in the web, waiting to pounce on intruders and dispose of them. Knowing her, I am sure this was done with great good humor — but firmly. Hans was endlessly hospitable, but even he could not have coped with all the curiosity seekers who came to see how an artist worked in the wilderness of Wyoming.

Ken and I could never keep up with Hans and Missy in square dancing. Whenever there were local competitions, those two were out on the floor — Missy's skirts whirling, Hans's hair flying. During the years, I watched it turn greyer but not perceptibly thinner. The

Blackbirds

Hans and "Missy" Kleiber as they attended one of the many exhibitions of his work. Most of them he did not attend.

134

last time I saw them whirl, Hans's hair was silvery white.

Hans's early working years had been spent on horseback, and when cars came into his life, he was a hopeless case. He was probably the worst driver in Wyoming, because he could not keep his eyes off the scenery and on the road. Seeing something that caught his attention, he drove straight toward it. After a few near disasters, he handed the car over to Missy and never touched the wheel again.

Hans's poetry came to light quite by accident. Rumaging through a desk drawer, he found a fat manila envelope containing poems, mostly composed while he was a forester and forgotten during the years of preoccupation with etching and painting. The poems were intimate reactions to his adventures, to his personal experiences, and most of all, to his surroundings. They were done on scraps of paper in camps, ranger cabins, trains, hotel rooms.

Publication never crossed Hans's mind. They were poems written as an outlet for his thoughts and feelings, often when he had no one to talk to. When a friend suggested that others would enjoy them, it never occurred to Kleiber to send his poetry to a publishing

Left: A ranch in the mountains

house. Being quite well known as an artist, he might well have found acceptance. As it was, he just took his poems to a local printer. The delightful little book has gone through numerous editions and is still available from the Mills Company in Sheridan, Wyoming.

For many years Hans had Christmas cards made for friends. These little gems are proudly framed in many homes across the nation. I have about twenty, and every once in awhile I give one to someone who can no longer acquire Kleiber etchings or paintings.

Hans's busy life went on until, in his late seventies, he began to be troubled by failing vision. He could no longer draw the exacting lines demanded by etching; but there was a great demand for hand-colored etchings, and this he was able to do for several years. Gradually other physical troubles came, and, since Missy was also ill and unable to care for him, the only answer seemed to be a nursing home.

His death at eighty was gentle as that of a falling leaf. I know, because I was the last person to see him alive. Missy, who died six weeks after Hans, was ill herself during his last days and could not come to see him often. Friends visited both whenever possible.

One December evening I stopped in just at dusk and found Hans sitting quietly in his wheelchair. It was too late, too dark and cold to wheel him out of doors, as I so often did, so I read to him. He was so ill that his mind

AN INDIAN SCOUT

An indian scout

136

Baldpates

137

sometimes wandered, and a dear friend, Dorothy Duncan, had suggested that we read to him "from his own book of poems," because these were parts of his life that he remembered. I found the book and began to read, and as we sat in the deepening dusk he took my right hand and held on. I turned the pages with my left, and as I rose to go those blue eyes looked up at me and he said, "I'd like to see you again." I answered, "Of course you will, Hans. I'll be back in a day or so." He did not reply — just shook his head.

I drove straight to my home, only five miles away, and as I entered the house, the phone was ringing. It was the head of the nursing home calling to tell me that when an attendant came to prepare Hans for supper she found him dead.

The leaf had fallen, but the memory of Hans will never dry up and wither for those who knew him. For those who did not know him, his spirit lives on in his pictures. The last poem read to him was one of his favorites:

TO MY BELL MARE*
The trail had skirted snow-flecked peaks all day,
And as it wound from rock-bound dell to dell,
I let the packtrain slowly pick its way
Behind the lead mare and her tinkling bell. . . .

As alpine night descended chill and damp,
The only sound that broke its witching spell
Came from the meadow, far below my camp,
Of horses grazing, and my lead mare's bell.

With scarce a break its cadence came and went,
As though she cropped the grass with measured ease,
Then it would, suddenly, the night air rent,
And fade again, when captured by a breeze.

Then, fitfully, her bell kept tinkling on
Until so faint and muffled came its sound,
The silvery rhythm from its peals had gone,
And it no more to man or earth seemed bound.

And when at last that night I fell asleep,
I dreamed a night wind stole its final ring
To hide it in some distant, star-lit keep
Beyond the reach of mortal ken or wing.

A book about an artist needs a critical evaluation by an expert. Because of his unusual qualifications, we have chosen Dr. James Forrest of the Art Department faculty at the University of Wyoming. He was one of the founders of the University Art Museum and currently its director. He teaches art at the college level and has judged numerous art exhibits across the United States. Dr. Forrest was formerly chairman of the Wyoming Council on the Arts and has, in the past, served as direc-

Songs, p. 59.

Right: Christmas in Dayton, Wyoming

138

Pintails feeding

140

Pintails loafing

Summer in the Rockies

The grouse hunter

tor of the Museum of New Mexico at Santa Fe and of the Gilcrease Museum of American History and Art in Tulsa, Oklahoma.

In the summer James Forrest is director of the Bradford Brinton Memorial Gallery in Big Horn, Wyoming, which houses a priceless collection of Western books and art, the latter including many Russell and Remington originals, as well as Kleiber etchings, watercolors, and oil paintings.

During those summers before Kleiber's death the two artists came to know each other well. Jim Forrest's presence meant a great deal to Hans because there were so few people here with whom he could discuss the technicalities of art. Much earlier (1912 to 1937) Kleiber talked often with Bill Gollings, another Wyoming artist, but only a few of those years encompassed the time when Hans was giving his full time to art.

When Dr. Forrest sent us his evaluation of Kleiber's work, he commented that he could have written about it from several different points of view. He chose the one he did because he had been so impressed with Kleiber's overpowering wish to portray the primitive world as he saw it, and by his early recognition that it was endangered. "In that sense," Forrest wrote, "Kleiber's vision was so much ahead of his time and so valid in the 1970s that I could not ignore it."

What Dr. Forrest says is an important reinforcement of what we had gleaned from Kleiber's work and the public response to it.

The Art of Hans Kleiber
by
James T. Forrest

The art of Hans Kleiber belongs to the long-standing tradition of America's concern for its own uniqueness as a land area, with its own varieties of animals, trees, and flowers. Artists began celebrating and documenting that uniqueness as early as the 16th century with Theodore de Bry's and John White's watercolors and engravings of life in the New World. From that time until the end of the last century, artists marched with, or ahead of, the frontiersmen across the continent. Most notable of these artist-naturalists were William Burtram, John James Audubon and his son, John Woodhouse, John Cassin, and others.

This was the tradition that inspired Hans Kleiber to record his own sector of the country — the region of the Big Horn Mountains in north central Wyoming.

As urbanization has increased, so has a growing awareness of the fragile condition of our remaining natural areas — those large and small sectors of our broad land composed of forest, swamp, stream, and plain which we somehow had thought would remain a constant, inviolate part of our heritage.

Titmice

Evening on the marshes

Man has been a strictly urban dweller for only brief moments in his long history on the earth. For a million years or more he was indeed as much a part of nature as the wild things all about him. He stood in awe of its forces — of storms, wind, rain, lightning, intense cold, extreme heat, and the miracles of the rising and setting of the sun and moon. Even the cities of the ancient civilized world, for the most part, were tied directly to the countryside for survival. It is a recent phenomenon, this divorcement of man from nature, and man is feeling both guilty and uncomfortable by his estrangement from the birthplace of his kind. This, and his need for the beauty, quiet, and solace to be found in natural surroundings, prompts man's present concern for the loss of much that once was considered an inexhaustible and constantly replenishing condition of this earth and especially of America, the New World.

Hans Kleiber, living as he did most of his life with nature, understood these longings of man to live in harmony with his environment, but he recognized also man's ignorance regarding the harm he could do in his attempt to "tame" nature. As a Forest Ranger he saw the hazards to wildlife when timber was carelessly harvested. He also saw the glory of man's concern when he properly understood the things of nature and bent his energies to protect and preserve these precious gifts. He watched a thousand sunsets and sunrises — often or-

chestrated by honking Canadian geese or formations of noisy mallards or teal; he lay in cover, sketching, as deer, elk, or moose grazed or stood alert. He watched rushing mountain streams in spring, fed by a million rivulets from retreating banks of melting snow, and he knew that the trout were beginning to search more eagerly for food; he watched the mountain birds of marvelous variety and habit as they flew from flower-bedecked meadows to the wind-sawn branches of tall pines and broad spruce. Hans understood nature's harshness, the life and death of all its separate parts, and its interdependence. He learned the names of the flowers, the trees, the birds, the wild animals, the rocks, the geological formations, and the structure of the mountain and plain — but he was much more than a cataloger of things; he understood them and respected their needs and deep meanings, not just for man but as part of a great plan — a universal scheme encompassing all things on and of the earth. This is what Hans Kleiber's art was about and how it was motivated.

Kleiber did watercolor, partly because it can be done easily in the field, but with varying skill. It was not his greatest strength. But he did produce a great number of fresh and delightful sketches of the Big Horns, as well as several carefully detailed watercolor and gouache paintings of wildlife and ranch scenes. He used oils, at first with the typical overmeticulous style of the un-

trained — for Hans was largely self-trained, and he experimented on his own, discovering, as he painted, methods and techniques which worked for him. But later, by the 1930s, he had achieved a very pleasing combination of brush and palette knife forte, of which there are several fine examples.

However, Kleiber was primarily a printmaker. He began with pure etching (the bitten line), added to this drypoint lines, and then discovered, with gratification, the warm tones possible by the use of aquatint (the use of a ground to produce the grain or shadings on a print). Finally he combined all of the above in some of his finest works. He also used a difficult, but not uncommon, method of toning — using colored inks in stages of printing from an aquatint plate to produce limited editions of beautiful color prints. Finally, Hans painstakingly hand-colored hundreds of prints during the last twenty years of his life — a time-consuming process of adding watercolor to previously printed etchings.

Unfortunately, during the last few years of Kleiber's life the strain of the close work incumbent on all etchers took its toll on his eyes; he could not see well enough to draw the lines on the waxed surface of the plates or to do the even more critical drypoint lines. He regretted this but found some solace in the coloring of the most popular of the prints he had pulled from the earlier plates. Even aquatint became too much for his diminished vision during the 1950s.

Hans Kleiber had considerable success and recognition during his lifetime, largely for his printmaking. His wildlife prints, Big Horn Mountain scenes, the historical series, and other subjects have found their way into collections of individuals and museums all across the country. But those who knew him recognized that his real reward came when the always-welcome visitor to his Dayton, Wyoming, studio saw in his work what he had tried so hard to put there — his own love of the mountain and stream, the birds, elk, and deer, the wild horses in blizzard or stomping from biting flies in summer, the changing nature of the sky from clear blue to the grey and white thunderheads over an expanse of broad land, the flocks of sheep quietly grazing in the upper mountain meadows.

Hans brightened and warmed to this recognition and felt a common bond with those who believed, as did Henry David Thoreau, that "In wildness is the preservation of the world."

Left: Winter scene
Courtesy Carolyn and James Forrest

Coming in

Fighting pheasants

Hans conveyed his own pleasure to others through pictures

Mildred Capron photo

Right: Village skating pond

H. Kleiber
Village Skating Pond — Dayton, Wyoming

Courtesy Mrs. Frank Horton